HOW TO DO A PHD THE (RELATIVELY) EASY WAY

Tips and tricks to navigate your PhD from one
student to another

Dr. J. C. Censin

How to do a PhD the (relatively) easy way

Tips and tricks to navigate your PhD from one student to another by Dr. J. C. Censin

Copyright 2021 by Jenny Censin

ISBN: 9798760341624

Cover design by Dr. Jenny Censin

Table of Contents

Foreword – read this first

In many ways, I was in an ideal position to start a PhD – or DPhil, as it is called at the University of Oxford. I was a 26-year-old medical doctor who had done two previous research projects in two different research groups, and both projects were highly related to my intended thesis topic. I knew that it would be challenging, but I also thought that I was very well prepared for it. Yet, my PhD journey turned out to be much more challenging than anything I had imagined, and I seriously considered quitting several times.

All doctorate students that I have met have struggled with *at least* one thing (but usually several) during their PhD. After I had submitted my thesis, I realized that there was a lot of advice that would have made my journey a lot easier if I had known about it before starting my program. There were also plenty of things that I was very grateful for that I had done from the start, things that I saw friends and colleagues struggle with. I therefore decided to write down these tips and tricks to help others avoid the worst pitfalls, from one PhD student to another.

I have deliberately written this book to be concise and easy to read, as if I was giving tips to a friend about to embark on the same journey. While it is written from my perspective as a Swedish PhD student working with large-scale genetic data at an English university, I am sure that all doctorate students will find something useful in the book. Still, some facts and advice may be incorrect or counterproductive for your specific situation. Rules, regulations, and norms differ between countries, universities, and fields, wherefore you need to look those up and adapt all advice for your particular situation. As always, think critically, and only implement the suggestions that would make your life easier. However, I would recommend that you read the entire book early on in your PhD, or even before starting your doctorate program. One of the key messages in the book is to plan for the end – the thesis and the viva – as early as possible, ideally even before you start applying for PhD positions. You can then return to specific sections as needed later.

Getting a PhD can be amongst the most growth-inducing challenges you can take on in life – both professionally and personally. It can be incredibly rewarding and satisfying to advance the barrier of human knowledge. That said – do not risk your health or well-being for it. A doctorate is not worth that level of sacrifice, and it is possible to get your PhD *and* be healthy and happy at the same time.

Best of luck!

Kind regards,

Dr. Jenny Censin

How to decide if, when, and where to do your PhD

What is a PhD?

A PhD is a doctorate degree, and (in most countries) the highest educational degree you can get. After completing a PhD, you will have the right to use the title "Doctor" in front of your name or add the letters "PhD", "Ph.D.", or "DPhil" after your name.

In many countries, you first need to obtain an undergraduate or bachelor's degree (usually three to four years) and a master's degree (commonly one to two years) before applying for PhD positions. In other countries, it is sufficient to have completed an undergraduate or bachelor's degree to apply for a PhD position.

There are large differences between PhD programs in different countries, universities, and fields. In some countries you are considered an employee and get paid a salary. In other countries, you are considered a student and have to pay for your studies (although there may be scholarships that you can apply for). At some universities and in some fields, you graduate after you have authored and defended a thesis that is based on a set number of scientific articles. At other universities and in other fields, you are not allowed to include previously published material in your thesis but must write a separate thesis. The differences in graduation requirements between countries, universities, and fields, means that the average time of a doctorate program can range between approximately three to seven years of full-time work.

The overarching structures of doctorate programs also vary considerable between research fields and countries. In the natural sciences, it is common that your overarching PhD project is divided up into several smaller research projects. Some supervisors may suggest that you only work on one research project at the time, whereas others may try and get you to juggle several from the start. Each research project will normally require you to do a set of experiments or collect data in some way, before analyzing the data and then writing up your findings in a research article and/or a thesis chapter. However, it is very common for research projects to fail for various reasons, and your entire PhD project might take a different direction than you had originally planned. On the contrary, some PhD students in the humanities may not have distinct research projects, but rather start to work on their thesis right away.

Good and bad reasons for starting a PhD

So, you have decided that you want to do a PhD. Why? Knowing the answer to this question – and questioning your motivation – is crucial before starting your PhD journey. Below I have listed some common reasons why people start doctorate programs, and things to consider:

1. "I do not know what else to do"

To me, this reason to start a PhD is similar to deciding to climb Mount Everest because you do not know what else to do. Completing a doctorate degree can be extremely challenging, and you will need to be highly motivated to finish it. If you do not know what else to do, consider getting a job in your field instead until you figure out what you want to do, and try and save some money. If you then decide to do a PhD you will have some savings before you start, and you will be better prepared to target your doctorate program for the post-PhD career that you want.

2. "I love XXX and would love to spend years studying it!"

This is a good reason to do start a doctorate program. However, be warned that many PhD students will go through periods when it feels like everything is going wrong and their passion for their topic vanishes. Yet, if this is your reason and you follow the advice in this book, you should have a good chance of having an enjoyable time during your PhD.

3. "I want to work in academia"

There can be a lot of glamour surrounding academia, and it is important to consider what a career in academia actually entails. While academic positions may offer more flexibility than certain other jobs, many fields and universities also have long working hours, (relatively) low pay, and poor job security. Many employment contracts are only one to two years long, and you may have to move country several times in the beginning of your career – whether that is a good or a bad thing depends on your personal preferences. Finally, it can be very difficult to succeed – you will be competing with a lot of very bright people for few job openings. Still, if you want to pursuit a career in academia, you will usually need a PhD.

4. "I want to have a high status or salary"

Having a doctorate may increase your chances of getting a high-status, well-paid job later, but do not take it for granted. In some fields and countries, your life earnings actually decrease by doing a PhD. If money is important to you, you may want to consider doing an undergraduate or master's degree in a highly sought-after field instead, such as medicine, engineering, or even trade schools for programming, electrical work, or plumbing (which may offer higher salaries than academia in some countries!).

5. "I want to learn the skills I would learn if I would do this PhD"

Personally, I think this is a good reason to start a doctorate program. In my case, I had trained as a medical doctor, but loved programming as a hobby. For me, doing a PhD was a way to combine those two skills and get a degree to show for it. In hindsight, it would have been a lot easier to just do an undergraduate in programming or data analysis instead, and it would probably have been just as easy to get a good job afterwards. Still, you do learn *a lot* from doing a PhD because of the fact that it is so challenging, and those skills are very valuable in life regardless of what you want to do later.

Think through your reasons to do a PhD very carefully. In my experience, one of the key reasons that many doctorate students warn other students not to start a doctorate program is because it is extremely difficult to quit once you have started. Even if you have spent years on your PhD, leaving before you are 100% finished may mean that you get no degree at all. Potential employers may wonder why you did not complete your PhD, so it may be more difficult to get a job than if you had not started a doctorate program in the first place. It is also common to have large debts because of high tuition fees and living costs, and these debts may be difficult to pay back if you cannot get a high-paying job. Finally, one of the main reasons why people drop out of doctorate programs is that it is so challenging that their mental health deteriorates to the point where they cannot continue. Thus, make sure that you know why you want to do a PhD before you start. You need to think that the

5

PhD is worth it even when all of your experiments are failing, your papers are being rejected, and it feels like you will never graduate.

Choosing what time in life to do a PhD

In some countries, you usually do a PhD right after you finish your undergraduate or master's degree. In other countries, it is common to have worked for a few years – even decades – before you begin a doctorate program. When you normally start your doctorate program can also depend on what field you are in and what background that you have. For example, it is not uncommon for medical practitioners to wait with doing a PhD until their forties or fifties. While it is rare that people deliberately wait to start a doctorate program, it is good to be aware of the pros and cons with doing a PhD in different stages in life.

Starting a PhD in your early twenties has several benefits. You usually have few other obligations, and you would typically not have had time to "get used" to a higher salary. You are used to studying, and you usually have a lot of energy. You might not have a problem with working long, irregular hours, and may not have a partner or kids at home with demands on your time. However, the downside with starting a PhD right out of school is that you have limited life experience. You will usually not have had time to build up a sense of self-worth in your job in the same way as if you are older. Even highly successful PhD students tend to feel like they are constantly failing or are not achieving enough. Having worked for a few years may have allowed you to build up a stronger sense of self-worth and professional competence. You may feel more comfortable standing up for yourself, if needed, and you will usually already have built up a professional and personal network that you can rely on. However, it can be difficult to return to being "a student". It can also feel disheartening when everybody around you is much younger. Oftentimes, there will be other claims on your time and money, and a large salary reduction could be impossible if you have a mortgage to pay and kids to support. Being older also means fewer working years left to reap any benefits of doing a PhD.

Deciding on country and university

Sometimes you do not have a choice in what country to do your PhD in for personal or professional reasons. However, there are certain things

6

that you should consider if you can choose which country to do your PhD in.

Doctorate program lengths vary between countries and universities but are usually between three to seven years. The main benefit with a shorter PhD is, obviously, that you will be done quicker. While you might be looking forward to starting your program now, it is common to be quite tired of it after a few years, and I am certain I would have dropped out if mine had been longer than three or four years. In addition, doing a shorter PhD means that you can enter the job market sooner, which in theory should increase your life earnings.

However, there are benefits of starting a longer doctorate program as well. If you want to stay in academia, a longer program means more time to publish articles, something that may give you an advantage when applying for grants or post-docs (the next career step in academia) later. In addition, many grants are only open for researchers within a certain time period after they graduate, so having more time to produce articles before that time limit is likely to give you a competitive advantage.

Some universities also offer the possibility to do a doctorate program part-time. In certain fields, it is common to do a PhD part-time while continuing to work part-time, for example in medicine. In some cases, keeping the connection with the job market may be mutually beneficial for both your PhD and your job. However, be aware that it will lengthen your time until graduation and may make it harder to keep your motivation and focus up. In addition, even if you are only technically supposed to work two half-time jobs, it often ends up being a lot more than 100% in total.

The graduation requirements also differ between countries and universities, as well as between departments/institutions. In some places, you need to have published (or be about to publish) a set number of articles to graduate, which you then combine into a thesis. In other places, you need to write an independent thesis to graduate (although you can usually publish articles as well, you just need to completely rewrite them for your thesis).

The main benefit with an article-based system is that published articles look good on your CV and will make it easier to get grants during and after your PhD. In addition, you also know how far along your PhD you

7

are. If you need 4 articles to graduate, you know that you are roughly half-way once you have two publications. The downside of the article-based system is that you can have bad luck when it comes to publishing articles. For example, if you end up with a bad research project or two that you cannot publish, the time that you have spent on those research projects will effectively be lost time in regards to the thesis (although you will of course have learned skills).

The main benefit of a having a non-article-based system is that you can often include null results or bad research projects in such a thesis. However, a major downside of a non-article-based system is that you may have to rewrite any published articles, which can be quite tedious. In addition, if you have not published any articles during your PhD, it may be harder to get grants and jobs after you graduate.

There are also other things to consider when thinking about what country and university to apply to. Salaries and scholarships differ a lot between countries. For example, PhD students in Sweden are considered employees and have employee rights and benefits. This would usually include a decent salary, payments towards retirement, a wellness grant, etc. On the contrary, PhD students in England are in most aspects considered students. That means that they are often technically required to pay tuition fees to do a PhD. While many doctorate students in England get scholarships to cover tuition fees and living costs, the scholarships tend to be quite low and only cover the basics. Hence, make sure to look up how it works in the countries that you are interested in and weight the pros and cons. In certain countries, it is also possible to do a PhD that is a collaboration between industry and a university, which could mean a higher salary and good chances of getting (or staying) employed by the company afterwards. You should also consider living costs in the city that the university is located – costs for a room or an apartment can vary a lot between cities and countries.

Certain universities may also offer remote-learning doctorate programs. While such an option may sound intriguing, beware of scams and know that it may mean considerably less support from supervisors and colleagues. If you are looking into part-time positions, also make sure that it actually part-time. In some places, it is common to employ part-time PhD students but expect them to work 100% or more.

You may also want to consider the following aspects when you choose a doctorate program:

1. Coursework

Some doctorate programs barely require any coursework to graduate, others require months or years of courses. You can normally take courses even if they are not required, but it may be difficult to get funding to attend courses if they are not mandatory. While mandatory courses tend to lengthen the PhD program, they can also help with expanding your professional network and broaden your knowledge of your field.

2. Teaching

In some countries, you normally have to teach undergraduates as part of your PhD. This will usually lengthen your PhD, but may be fun, boost your CV, and give you extra money. However, usually there will be teaching opportunities even if teaching is not required.

3. Research groups

Some doctorate programs require that you try out several research groups before settling on one, others that you stay in the same research group your entire PhD. On one hand, doing rotations in different research groups can translate into a longer PhD, as the work you do in the other research groups may not be possible to include in your thesis. On the other hand, trying out different research groups may increase your chances of finding the supervisor and research group that maximizes your chances of a smooth PhD, which may speed up the process in the long run.

4. Number of supervisors

At some departments/institutions you just have one supervisor, at other departments/institutions you will have several supervisors as well as a thesis committee. For more information about this, see the "Choosing the right supervisor and research group" section.

5. Examinations

At some universities, you have to pass several examinations along the PhD journey, at others there may only be one examination at the end. Most students would probably say that they want as few examinations as

9

possible. However, examinations are a great way to make sure that you are on track and to identify and correct any problems as early as possible.

6. Decisions on PhD projects

For some doctorate programs, you are responsible to decide on the exact research question and how you will answer it. In other places, potential supervisors suggest projects which you then apply for as a part of your program application. Which alternative that is best is probably down to personal preference. Deciding on a project yourself is likely to give you more freedom, but it can be difficult to come up with a good project if you have limited experience in the field.

7. Possibilities to change field

In some countries, you always continue in the same field that you did your undergraduate or master's degree in. In other countries, it might be possible to radically change between fields as disparate as music, math, and biology.

8. Language

Before you decide on which country to do your PhD in, you may want to consider any language barriers. English is more and more becoming the main language at universities, but not all academics speak good English, and you may have to learn the local language to be able to communicate well with your supervisor. Having to learn another language before you can communicate with your supervisor or integrate in the local community can be tough, so consider this aspect before choosing what country to do your PhD in.

9. Recognition of your degree

Some employers regard degrees obtained abroad as "better" than degrees obtained within the country, but for other employers it may be the complete opposite. In general, whether a "foreign" degree is better or not than a more local one will depend on the country you want to work in later. It will also depend on which university you got your degree from. Some universities may be very well-recognized within the country, but largely unknown abroad.

Selecting a good field and PhD project

How much flexibility you have in choosing your field and PhD project depends on what country, university, and field that you are doing your doctorate in. In some countries, you can change fields completely between your undergraduate degree and your doctorate program, in other countries you will be limited to the field that you already have a degree in. Still, it is almost always possible to slightly change direction within a field. For example, by looking at the ethical aspects of something in your field you might get a more "humanistic" PhD, whereas by developing methods in your fields you might get a more "mathematical" PhD.

As you consider different fields and PhD projects, I would encourage you to try and get to know the field before you make a final decision. In ideal scenarios, you may have done your undergraduate or master's in the field, maybe even with the same supervisor as you will have for your PhD. If this is not the case, perhaps you can work as a research assistant for a summer to get to know the field (and a potential supervisor) before making a final decision? If that is not possible, perhaps you could reach out to potential supervisors (see the section "Finding a good supervisor and research group") and ask if you could work alongside a junior group member for a few days? If that is not possible either, for example due to health and safety regulations, I would encourage you to try and talk to a more junior member in the field to hear about what their daily life is like. Some other aspects you may want to think about include:

1. What skills do I want to learn?

This is a crucial question if one of your reasons for doing a PhD is to improve your chances of getting certain jobs in the future. For example, I wanted to improve my programming skills and learn how to work with big data, as I like working with data and knew that those skills were in high demand on the job market. I therefore decided to do a PhD project where I would do big data analysis of medical data, which essentially combined my medical degree with my programming hobby.

Think about what skills you would learn by doing the different PhD projects that you are considering and consider how those skills match the jobs that you would like to have in the future.

2. What skills do I enjoy learning and doing?

11

You will spend several years doing the methods that are required for your field and PhD project. If you dislike doing lab experiments, you will likely hate having to do it for years. Try to find a good match between what skills you enjoy doing and what skills will be required for your PhD project.

Sometimes you may not have done the kind of work that your PhD project would require before. If there is no possibility to spend some time in the lab of your prospective supervisor, you can try and compare the daily PhD work with more basic tasks that you have done before. For example, if your PhD project would require following a lot of very complicated lab protocols that take eight hours, what are your feelings towards following complicated baking recipes taking a similar length of time? Although it will obviously not be exactly the same, your feelings towards the more basic task may give you an idea about what you would think about the day-to-day tasks you would be doing.

3. What are the related things I would have to do for this PhD project?

Will your PhD project require extensive traveling? Will it require coming into the lab every six hours for a week every month? Will it require working nights? Will it mean that you cannot have extended time off because of cells or animals that need feeding? Will you have to perform experiments on research animals?

Think about the daily tasks that your field and/or PhD project would require you to do. Are you okay with doing them for the next couple of years?

4. What are the back-up alternatives in case things go wrong?

For some PhD projects, there might be plenty of other professors at the university that could step in as supervisors, if needed. Such a need could arise for several reasons – because you do not get along with your supervisors, or because your supervisor decides to change job or even dies. For other PhD projects, you might rely on a single, expensive machine – what are your alternatives if that one breaks? Usually, the university would help you in these cases, but it might be good to think through such scenarios beforehand. Even if you decide that you want to use that single, expensive machine in your PhD project, perhaps you could tweak the project slightly so that you also have the opportunity to do research projects that are not dependent on the machine in case it would break for six months.

5. Is this an easy or a hard PhD project?

When you decide on your overarching PhD project, most projects will be somewhere on the scale "high risk and high reward" or "low risk and low reward". Choosing a PhD project where you try to solve an important problem that nobody has been able to solve before fits into the first category. You would be at high risk of finishing your PhD without having solved the problem and without any publications, but if you manage to solve the problem, you will have made a name for yourself. PhD projects that fall in the "low risk and low reward" category tend to be projects that look at applying established methods on a new dataset, disease, or where some other variables have changed. If you have a good research question, a project can often be published even if you have null results, although maybe not in the most prestigious journal. Low risk and low reward PhD projects may also involve research questions that fewer researchers are working on. For example, there is high competition in research involving diseases like cancer or heart disease, but much fewer researchers work with rare disorders like sclerosteosis. Strong competition in a field may also translate into a higher risk of being "scooped", that is, that somebody publishes a study so similar to yours that it cannot be published. On the other hand, if you do find some novel and revolutionary results for cancer or heart disease, you are more likely to get your article into a prestigious journal than if you are working on a much rarer disease.

For most prospective PhD students, I would recommend trying to go for an easy project. A PhD is hard enough as it is. If you get a few articles published you will likely be able to get a post-doc somewhere, even if the articles are not revolutionary. If you are very smart, very passionate about your topic, and want to make a name for yourself, you can consider going for a harder project, but make sure that you have a good idea of what you are getting yourself into. I would also recommend that you have a back-up plan. Overarching PhD projects are usually split into several smaller research projects, so it may be possible to have one high-risk, high-reward research project and several low-risk, low-reward research projects as a back-up (see the section "Research projects" for more information).

Finding a good supervisor and research group

Choosing the right supervisor is probably the most important factor when doing a PhD. I cannot stress this enough – your supervisor can make or break your PhD and your career. At the same time, it is incredibly difficult to know whether a supervisor would be a good fit for you or not. Below, I have listed a few things to consider to increase your chances of a good supervisory fit:

1. Number of supervisors

In some PhD programs, the supervisory arrangement is very fixed, with each student having a set number of supervisors from start to finish. In other programs, the number of supervisors for each student can vary considerably, and supervisors are commonly added or removed over the years. Supervisory structures can also vary from vague (where it is unclear who has final say) to clearly outlined, with for example one main supervisor, one secondary supervisor, and three other researchers making up a thesis committee that reviews the student's progress each year.

In general, having more supervisors will mean that you have a stronger back-up system if it does not work out with one of your supervisors, but it also means that more people must get along. After having talked to friends and colleagues, I got the general impression that one supervisor works very smoothly as long as he or she is knowledgeable, remains at the department/institution your entire PhD, and you get along well. However, if there are any problems – even just your supervisor being long-term sick – you have no immediate back-up solution. If you have two supervisors, you have some back-up but is still easy to keep both supervisors informed and meet with them regularly. Three supervisors or more seems to easily cause disagreements, as there is then a total of six inter-personal relationships that need to work. In addition, just arranging supervisory meetings that three senior researchers or more can attend could be quite tricky. Still, just because a person is listed as a supervisor on a paper does not necessarily mean that you will ever even meet them, and at the end of the day it is the number of *involved* supervisors that matter. In addition, remember that it is not just you who needs to get along with your supervisors, but your supervisors also need to get along with each other. Ideally, having supervisors that have worked together before is probably a safer choice than some that have never met previously.

2. Seniority

A major benefit of a more senior professor is that they have usually supervised PhD students several times before and hopefully know what they are doing. Other people in the field know who they are, which might help you when you apply for jobs if you are staying in academia. They often have more money from grants, which might translate into more money for courses and conferences for you. The downside with a more senior professor is that they usually have less time for each individual student. Sometimes that will mean that you will be left to fend for yourself, other times somebody else in the group will be assigned an informal supervisory role. The benefits of a more junior supervisor is basically the opposite to those of a senior professor. Junior supervisors tend to be more hands-on, sometimes even still doing actual research experiments themselves. They are also more dependent on you succeeding since they are in the early stages of their career, which can translate into more help for you.

3. Background

A common misconception among junior PhD students is that their supervisor knows everything. Whereas this can be the case, quite often professors will also get graduate students to work in an area that they themselves are less familiar with, or two professors may hire a PhD student as a "collaborating link" between their two fields and research groups. In general, I would recommend making sure that your professor has worked in the area that your doctorate project will be in. It will save you a lot of wasted time if your supervisor can point you in the right direction as you go along and already know which research projects are likely – and less likely – to be worth pursuing. I would recommend you to think twice before starting a PhD project that both you and your supervisor are unfamiliar with. While such projects can be exciting, you will have a very steep learning curve in the beginning and very little help. Similarly, be cautious about accepting a PhD position where you will be the link between two different fields and two different research groups. While such research can be very exciting, your supervisors may not be able to help you if they cannot understand half of your project.

4. Way of working

Some supervisors will give you deadlines, others will not. Some will meet you twice a week and work alongside you in the lab, others you will not see during your entire PhD. Some will demand that you work regular hours, some would not bat an eyelid if you went on vacation for three months without telling anybody. Some will tell you exactly what to do each day, others will just want you to report results every six months.

Knowing whether a supervisor is a good fit or not is about knowing what you need to succeed. The main benefit of a very involved professor that tells you exactly what to do is that it probably makes your PhD a lot easier (if they know what they are doing). The downside of a very involved professor is that you may not learn how to find information and think critically yourself. I have met people that had been quite successful in their PhDs, but that had never learned to think for themselves. It then became too challenging for them when they started post-docs in labs with less involved professors. If you have a supervisor that just gives you general instructions and then leave you to figure it out, you will learn a lot. You will have a much harder time, but if you can manage you will have learned skills that will be incredibly useful for life. In general, having a supervisor who is somewhere between the two extremes may be a good compromise between learning the skills that you need, having a life during your PhD, and actually managing to graduate.

Finally, supervisors may also differ in other regards that may be worth considering. Will your prospective supervisors encourage and pay for you to attend courses and conferences? Will they require you to work certain hours or are they more flexible, and which option do you need to get work done? Will they respond to e-mails quickly or does each e-mail require five chaser e-mails? Will they travel all the time, or will they be doing experiments in the lab themselves? Will they suggest that you work on multiple research projects at the same time, or one at a time? Once again, you must know what you need in order to choose the right supervisor for you.

Obviously, you can probably not ask your potential supervisors how they normally behave regarding all of these aspects. The absolute best situation is if you have already worked with your potential supervisor, for example if you have done your master's thesis with them. Then you will already know the pros and cons of working with them, and if it is a good supervisory fit. If that is not possible, you need to get objective and honest information from students who have worked or are working with your potential supervisor. You can often just ask your potential supervisor if you could get the names of some previous PhD students, or you could do some detective work online by looking at the research group's website or previous theses that list your potential supervisor as a supervisor. Then, reach out to the students and ask if you could meet up or have a video call. Ideally, you want to talk to some PhD students that have already finished, since they will have gone through all the PhD stages with the potential supervisor and might be able to speak more freely. You may also want to try and have an informal conversation with current PhD students without the supervisor present. However, be aware that they might not feel able to give you their honest opinion, so read between the lines! Do they hesitate when you ask about how much support they are getting? Do they answer with "it's okay" when you ask them about the atmosphere in the group? You may get more honest answers if you start the conversation with saying that you will treat anything that they say as strictly confidential. Needless to say, you should regard any negative information that the students give you as strictly confidential and not betray their trust.

5. Group size

Some research groups are just you and the supervisor, others can be up to 70 people or more (something that also varies a lot by field). Larger research groups mean that the professor will need to split his/her time between more people, which may mean less face-to-face time for you. On the other hand, you have more colleagues to reach out to for help and your post-PhD network will be larger.

6. Personality

You will hopefully work very closely with your supervisor for a long time. It is probably a bit too much to hope for that you will be best friends, but it might be good if there is at least a decent personality fit.

Finally, remember that it is common that supervisors assign students "informal" supervisors, usually a post-doc in the lab. In this case, it is often more important that the fit with the informal supervisor works than the fit with the official supervisor. If you get to meet the potential supervisor before deciding on a PhD, make sure that you ask who you would work with on a day-to-day basis and try and get to meet that person.

Money matters

PhD salaries and scholarship are almost always very low. However, the amount of money that you get – if you even get any – can differ vastly between different countries, universities, and research groups. In some places, you might also have to pay tuition fees. I would caution against accepting a PhD position where you are not paid enough to cover your tuition fees and living expenses. You are doing real work and that should be recognized. When considering the amount of money that you will be paid, also consider how much your living expenses will be.

It might also be worth investigating if there is additional money that you can apply for. You may be eligible for extra scholarships from the university, non-profit organizations, companies, or the government. The university library and any student finances office should be able to suggest good places to start looking for suitable scholarships and remember to ask fellow students as well.

At some universities, you can also make extra money from teaching, or it may be possible to have a job on the side. If possible, I would recommend trying to avoid having a budget that relies on you working extra, since that will take time and energy away from your PhD. If you must work, consider trying to find a job that is in a related field and that gives you valuable experience (in addition to being fun and paying well). Finally, supervisors may be able to give you extra funding or even fund you completely from their grants, so remember to ask if appropriate.

How to get a PhD position

The process for applying for doctorate programs differ between countries and universities but often includes a combination of sending in your CV and/or grades, some sort of motivation or cover letter, an essay or a research proposal, and interviews. In addition, there are "informal" parts to the application process that can greatly enhance your chances of getting a PhD position.

Reach out to your potential supervisors

One of the key things to get accepted to a PhD program is to make sure that your potential supervisor(s) want you to join their research group(s). If the application process is done by applying to a program (as opposed to directly to the supervisors), strongly consider reaching out to your potential supervisors beforehand (unless it is against the regulations). Write a very polite e-mail asking for a meeting and remember to use the potential supervisor's correct title. Before that meeting, make sure that you have looked up your prospective supervisors and know what they are working on. Prepare a few questions beforehand and consider politely asking them if you could get feedback to help you through the application process (unless it is against any regulations). You will greatly increase your chances of being accepted if your potential supervisors are helping you through the application process. Do not underestimate the power of having a professor on your side. At many universities, you will be almost guaranteed acceptance if your prospective supervisor is vouching for you.

CV and grades

Some universities have minimum requirements for grades, but you can often apply even if you do not meet the criteria as universities may make exceptions. If you have a very good reason as to why your grades are too low, you can consider explaining the situation in the cover letter but consider the local culture before doing so. Valid excuses for low grades could be severe illness, being a primary caregiver (official or unofficial), or death in the family. Also, remember that the application processes differ between universities and countries. For example, in my experience Swedish universities tend to care much less about grades and more about other aspects. Hence, if your grades are too low to be accepted at some universities, consider applying to universities in other countries and/or boosting other aspects of your CV.

You need your CV to look outstanding, and you need to make sure that you follow the CV culture in the country that you apply in as it can vary dramatically between countries. Some of the things that can differ are the length of a CV, how much personal information (such as marital status) that you should share, and whether you should include a photo or not. Rather than winging it, I suggest finding CVs of people at the university (or from another university in that country). You can often find CVs on the departmental websites. If not, you can look up the names of the people in the research group that you will apply to on LinkedIn or similar websites and you will often find their CVs there. Look at several CVs and then use a similar layout as the best ones. Make sure to get feedback from other people after you have written your CV. Ideally, it is great if you can get a more senior person in academia's thoughts on it. Many universities also offer CV workshops for their students, so you can also check with your current or previous university if they have some sort of career services that you could ask for help. So, what do you generally want to include in your CV?

1. Education

You primarily want to include courses and programs from universities and colleges. If you do not have a lot of other things to pad your CV with, you may in certain cases want to include your grades from high school/A-levels, but this is dependent on culture and personal preference. You can also include what grade average you received in your previous degrees.

2. Work experience

Ideally you want to include relevant work experience. Have you taught during your undergraduate? Any relevant summer jobs? It may be worth including a brief description of your previous jobs and how the skills you learned at those jobs are relevant for a PhD position. If you have a lot of relevant work experience, consider putting the work experience section above the education section on your CV.

3. Publications

Make sure to include references to any scientific publications that you have contributed to. Professors often take on PhD students because they want them to produce work that can be published. Previous publications make you stand out as a candidate. Even if an article has not been submitted, you can write the suggested article name, the author list, and then "soon to be submitted to ..." and the name of the journal you plan to submit to. Similarly, if you have already submitted a paper and it is currently under review, you can write "currently under review in ..." and then the journal name.

4. Other categories

There are other categories that you may want to include. For example, you can have a section called "skills", where you can list any skills that you have that are relevant for the PhD position. You can also include a section with any poster presentations and if you have been invited to hold talks at conferences. You can also have an "additional information" section where you include things like volunteering experiences, exam results, citizenship, and if you fulfill any necessary visa requirements. Finally, in some countries it is common to include contact information to your references, but make sure to confirm that your references are happy to give you a reference first.

5. Contact information

You want to make it as easy as possible for anybody to contact you. Professors will often print out your CV, and it is easy for your CV pages to get separated. Therefore, consider including your contact information on each page, for example in a footer.

A few more things to consider when you make your CV:

1. Have very little text on your CV and make sure it is very easy to read

PhD admittance boards or professors will often have to go over tens, or even hundreds, of CVs. Many professors will not look at a CV for more than a minute or two at a first glance. Make sure that they get all the key arguments for why you should be accepted in less than a minute! In many countries, CVs should not be longer than 1-2 pages (although full academic CVs may be considerably longer if they include a large number of publications).

2. Only include relevant information

Given that you want the most important information to come across immediately, only include relevant information. One strategy that I have used is to exclude the least relevant information until I have a CV that is about 1-2 pages.

3. Use standard "gradings" whenever possible

Use standard gradings of your skills whenever possible. For example, for languages you can use the Common European Framework of Reference for Languages (CEFR) levels (A1-C2) instead of using words like "basic" and "fair", which can mean very different things to different people.

4. Make it as easy for your references as possible

Normally, you will be asked to submit two to three references. Sometimes, you will be asked to submit letters of recommendation when applying for PhD positions. Other times, you provide contact information to your references, and then the admittance board or the potential supervisor calls them. Regardless, you want to make it as easy as possible for your references.

First of all, ask your potential references if they could consider being your reference. Ideally, it should be senior, well-known academics that you have a professional relationship with. Great references could be any professors or post-docs that you did your undergraduate project(s) with and that you know think highly of you. If you are choosing between asking a famous professor who barely knows who you are and a junior researcher that knows you well, many people would recommend that you ask the more senior professor. Personally, I would recommend that you consider including both as references. If you have job experience, you can also consider asking your boss, even if it is in an unrelated field. Tread carefully if there is any risk that your references have a negative view of you. Many references would say "no" if they cannot give a positive reference or say that they would feel obliged to inform about whatever it is that they do not like about you. However, sometimes they may just seem unenthused or try to avoid being your reference. If this is the case, strongly consider asking somebody else.

You want to tell your references what kind of job or position you are applying to, and potentially what they are looking for in a candidate. This will help your references highlight your strengths specific to the position. You should also ask if there is anything you can do to help. For example, you could offer to give your references a list of your achievements. Some references might also suggest that you write a first draft of the letter of recommendation for yourself. In these cases, do a thorough job and do not be too modest! Your reference should change things as they seem fit. In these cases, make sure that you ask your references to write the recommendation with plenty of time to spare. If you are in charge of the letter submission, you can consider giving them a "false" deadline a week or so before the true deadline, but only if there is no risk of them finding out that you have lied to them. It is very common that references write their recommendations in the absolute last minute, so you want to minimize the risk of the letters being too late. You can also consider giving your references polite reminders until they have been submitted.

If you are just supposed to send your references' contact information, make sure that you notify your references before the potential supervisor or admittance board might call. Remind your references about the position that you are applying for. Also make sure to inform both the reference and any person who makes the call about any name changes. It can be very confusing for both the reference and the supervisor/admittance board if you have gotten married and they know you under different names. In certain cases, you may also need to consider culture or language barriers. In some cultures, references should be absolutely sparkling with praise, in other cultures such a reference would be regarded as untrustworthy. If you can, ask for help from somebody with experience with the local culture or do some research online. In the case of a severe language barrier, I would recommend talking to a student admission administrator about how best to proceed.

Finally, inform your references how it went after you are done with the application process and consider sending a thank you-note or even some flowers (depending on the culture).

Cover letters and personal statements
You want your cover letter and/or personal statement to stand out. If you are unsure about how to do it, or if there are large cultural differences,

consider reaching out to people that you know or students at the university you are applying to. Normally, there will be social media groups specific to a university, and you can simply beg for people's previous graduate applications there or tips and tricks for what this particular admittance board seems to be looking for. Obviously, you should not plagiarize their writing, but rather use it as a template to see how you can organize your own. There are also many country-specific templates available online if you just search for e.g. "German cover letter", but remember to be critical of the source.

Whether or not your application is in your native language or a secondary one, make sure that you have somebody read it over. If you do not know anybody that can help you with that, check with your university. Universities often have career services that can help with looking over your CV and/or cover letters, even for alumni.

Just like with CVs, one of the key things with a cover letter or a personal statement is to keep them brief. I would normally recommend cover letters to be below a page unless the application guidelines (or local norms) say otherwise.

Essays and research proposals

At universities where you are applying through a standardized process, you will often be required to either write an essay or a research proposal based on your suggested PhD project. As a first step, I would strongly recommend that you try and get your hands on some other essays or research proposals to use as a template. For example, you could ask your potential supervisor, the students in their research group that you (hopefully) talked to when deciding on a research group or reach out in social media groups for that university. An essay or research proposal that was part of a successful application is a great template when you write your own.

To write a good essay/research proposal, you need to know the field that you will write about. To do this, your first task is to find a good academic database – a database where you can search for scientific articles – for your field. The "best" academic database depends on your field – consider searching online or asking a librarian if you do not know which one is most suitable (some examples are Google Scholar and PubMed).

The next step is to search the academic database for key words in your suggested topic + "review". A review article gives an overview of a field and will give you a lot of information in a short amount of time. Scroll through the results until you see one that seems to be about your topic – ideally one that has been cited many times before (you can often select to see the number of citations for an article). If the title seems promising, read the abstract in detail. If the article seems to be what you need, you will need to get access to the article, which can be a bit problematic as a lot of articles are behind paywalls. In my field, there has been a push in recent years to try and make more articles open access, but unfortunately a lot of articles are still pay-to-read. Universities commonly subscribe to a lot of journals and give free access to them for their students, commonly through virtual private networks or if you physically sit in their library. If you do not belong to a university, you may want to check with your local library or even any local university library and ask nicely if there is any way for you to be allowed to access articles through them. If none of these options work for you, you can either pay for the article, or write your essay based on open-access articles only.

After you have found a good review article, read it through and make sure to save it if it seemed useful. Repeat as needed until you have a good grasp of the topic you will be heading into.

If you are supposed to write a research proposal, you will also need to come up with a good research question and describe what methods you will use. Sometimes, you can find suggestions on future research in the discussion section of both original research and review articles. Another great shortcut is to find a few recent theses in your field, ideally from your suggested supervisor's research group or a related group. You can often find them for free at the university library website or just politely ask the author or supervisor for it. If you read the discussion section of the theses, the student will often have listed potential new research avenues to build on their work. Given that the student will have spent a few years in the field, their suggestions are likely to be at least decent. In addition, if you use this approach, you will usually find a great overview of the field in the thesis introduction. The student may even have described suitable methods to answer the research question, which would make your job even easier. Just remember to give the student credit if you use this approach – you do not want to start your PhD with plagiarizing. Of course, you could also try and come up with your own research question and do research about suitable methods. However, it can be very difficult to come up with good research questions when you have limited experience of research. Regardless of how you come up with your research question, try and get feedback on your suggestions from your potential supervisor or an experienced researcher in your field, if allowed. They should be able to find any obvious problems with your idea and suggested method.

Thereafter, you need to start writing the essay or research proposal. Make sure that you cite all the information that you include. To help with that, you can download a reference manager – some common reference managers are Mendeley, EndNote, Zotero, and Paperpile. Some reference managers are free, others you have to pay for, but if you belong to a university they may subscribe to some that you are also free to use. Instead of referencing review articles, try and reference the articles that the review is referencing (ideally you should reference original research, not reviews).

Once you feel that your essay or research proposal is polished, make sure to get feedback on it from friends, family, colleagues, former teachers, or potentially any career services that you have access to. If it is not against the application regulations, you should also consider asking your prospective supervisors if they can give you feedback. Having a professor look over your essay or research proposal could very well make the difference between acceptance and rejection.

Interviews
Depending on the university, department/institution, and supervisor, you may have one or several interviews of varying degrees of formality. Oftentimes you will be asked to give a presentation. Commonly, you will be asked to either do a presentation about yourself, about a previous research project that you have done, or about the PhD project that you will start on. So, how do you ace these?

First of all, carefully consider the instructions given. What should the presentation be about? How long should it be, and does that include time for questions? Thereafter, make a presentation outline and consider the depth that you should go into. It is crucial that the length of your presentation is within the suggested time limit, especially if you will give the presentation for an admittance panel where interviews are often conducted back-to-back. If you exceed your allotted time, an admittance panel may simply cut you off when your time is out.

For research projects, the classic structure is to go through the background/introduction, then the methods, then the results, and then potentially have a short discussion slide, just like a normal research article. It is also common to end with a quick summary. You can also do a very short one-slide version of the classic research project presentation – just have a bullet point for each section.

You have a lot of flexibility if you are to give a presentation about yourself. While you can include some fun facts about yourself in such a presentation, most such presentations that I have seen will still be primarily about your education, previous jobs, and some key research project. Depending on the culture, these presentations can often be a bit more "fun", and it can then be clever to include some fun fact about you to make them remember you.

For all your slides, make sure that you have a consistent layout. Keep them minimalistic and write very short bullet points rather than complete sentences. Similarly, it is usually a good idea to have one larger image than a lot of smaller ones (and images are great to include overall). Try to have one message per slide and make the header declarative. For example, instead of having "Background" as the header, you could have "The pathophysiological mechanisms to post-COVID are unclear".

In general, more inexperienced presenters usually try and include way too many words in a PowerPoint slide. Cut it down as much as you possibly can. Whether you should write down your talk and rehearse until you know it by heart, or just make sure that you can talk from the bullet points, is up to you. In my experience, different approaches work best for different people, so do what suit you best. However, do not read from a script and make sure you have a natural flow if you have learned an entire script. For more tips and tricks about acing a presentation, see the "Giving talks" section.

Practice answering standard job interview questions as well as questions based on your past and suggested research – I have included some example PhD interview questions in the appendix. It is very common to be asked highly detailed questions about your previous research projects, so be sure to refresh your memory if needed! You could also consider having a "mock interview" with friends, family, or colleagues before your interview. For certain prestigious universities, you can find examples of common interview questions if you search online. Try and reply correctly but succinctly. If you do not understand a question, ask for clarification. If you do not know the answer to a question, make that clear, but continue with something like "based on this and that, I would think that it's this and that". If you have absolutely no clue, it is usually best just to admit that in a calm manner and without acting embarrassed or nervous. If you are in a country where titles are used, make sure that you address the people interviewing you with the correct title. If you do not know what their titles are, it is usually better to address them by a higher-ranking title.

Adapt your attire to the culture in the country that you are applying to. It is usually better to be dressed too formally than too informally. In general, put on – at least – a formal shirt and dress pants, a skirt, or similar. In my experience, jeans are very rarely a good idea, but might be acceptable in very informal countries where you are having a very informal meet-up with your potential supervisor. However, it would rarely be wrong to have a pair of slacks/skirt, a shirt, and a suit jacket, so consider playing it safe. In addition, do not forget the details – a belt if appropriate, appropriate shoes, and give any bags and jackets a thought.

Finally, make sure that you get a good night's sleep before the interview, that you know exactly where you are going for the interview and allow for delays getting there.

How to excel at the practical aspects of a PhD

Setting up your daily life as a PhD student

You have gotten your acceptance letter and are hopefully eager to get started. However, besides spending time on the actual research, you should also dedicate time and effort to setting yourself up for an easy and successful PhD:

1. Plan ahead

The main message in this book is to plan ahead. As early as possible in your PhD, familiarize yourself with your university's PhD regulations so that you know what you need to have accomplished by the end of your PhD to be allowed to graduate. Then, make a solid plan to achieve those aims as easily as possible. I will return to this point in many sections of this book, but this is the foundation to having an easy and successful PhD. Know what you need to achieve, plan for it, and try to make it as failure-proof as possible by foreseeing potential problems before they arise.

2. Routines

For most PhD students, the easiest way to optimize both productivity and well-being is to establish good routines and habits. First, you need to think about when and under what circumstances that you work best. Are you most productive in the morning, afternoons, or evenings? Do you work better if you take a 15-minute break every hour or does it suit you better to take a longer lunch break and go for a run? Are those two extra hours that you work in the evening actually productive or are they just wearing you down?

I would encourage you to carefully think through how to organize your daily life so that you optimize both productivity and well-being. For example, I realized that I could only be productive about six to eight hours each day. If I worked more one day, my productivity the next day suffered. I therefore created a routine for myself where I worked approximately 8 am to 4:30 pm each weekday, with a 30-minute lunch break. Since I knew that I would be working these hours no matter what, there was no room for procrastination or staying home just because I did not feel like working. In addition, I felt that I could properly let go of work on my spare time.

3. Time off

Remember to schedule time off work on a daily, weekly and yearly basis. Your productivity will only go up with the number of hours that you work up to a certain point. Thereafter, your productivity will go down. Do not be fooled into spending more and more time working to try and increase your output – it will often have the complete opposite effect as you make more mistakes and detours.

I would suggest having an absolute minimum of one day off per week, no matter how stressful things get. That way, you will always get a minimum amount of complete rest, and if you know that you are always free on, for example, Saturdays, it becomes much easier to mentally let go of work that day. I would also strongly recommend not checking your e-mail or other work tools on your time off unless you absolutely must. Even if it only takes a few minutes to respond to an e-mail, it will make you start thinking about work, so that the actual amount of time you are thinking about work is much longer for each e-mail. Finally, allow yourself a proper vacation at least once a year to recharge your batteries.

4. Organize your time and keep track of what you have done

Whichever field that you are in, it is important that you find some way to organize your work. Personally, I favored a very simple system. I had a simple document on my computer with a to-do list at the bottom. Every day, I wrote today's date at the end of the document before the to-do list. When I had completed something, I wrote it up under today's date. I also wrote up any key thoughts or insights I had had that day. If I read an article or found a webpage with good information, I wrote it up in this journal, as well as any supervisory meeting notes. At the end of my PhD, this journal was over 200,000 words, and I was extremely grateful for it. Before my exams at the end, I could just skim through it in a couple of days and refresh all the insights I had had during my PhD. I could also refresh my memory as to why I had chosen this or that method, which helped me in my thesis defense.

My to-do list kept having things added, so every now and then I went over it and pruned it down to the essential things. At the end of each day,

I also wrote up what I was going to do the next day. That way, it was easy to get started each morning and on Mondays after the weekend.

However, this approach will likely not suit everybody. Some people will be required to fill out official lab journals, in which case it might be easier to write down all thoughts and insights there. There are also more fancy, digital planning/journal tools with advanced timelines, subtasks, etc., that you might prefer. However, it might be good to consider having an informal journal as well where you can write down information that you do not want others to see. For example, the names of your supervisor's kids or your impression of professors that you meet, which can help later when you need to decide on examiners or when you are looking for your next job.

Whichever system that you have, make sure that it is backed-up. For this reason, I would advise against having a hand-written journal. Also, it is crucial that any sensitive data is stored in a safe way and in accordance with data storage protocols.

In essence, make sure that you have some sort of daily plan, and some sort of way to keep track of your thoughts and what you have done. In addition to the benefits I have already highlighted, this system also means that whenever you feel that you are not getting anything done, you can look back and remember all the things that you have accomplished.

5. Divide big tasks up into small tasks

As the popular saying goes, a PhD is a marathon and not a sprint, and it is very easy to get disheartened when you compare what you have completed to what you have left to do. To combat these feelings, divide big tasks up into smaller tasks. For example, instead of having the daunting point "write the thesis" on your to-do list, have "write 1,000 words" or "write the introduction to chapter 2". Then, write up both big and small accomplishments in your lab journal when you achieve them. It will help you feel accomplished and minimize the risk of giving up or starting to procrastinate. Also, remember to properly celebrate any milestones along the way, such as articles being accepted or passing any half-way exams.

6. Get to know the other people in your group/lab/department/institution/field

There are many benefits to getting to know the people around you. First of all, it can be fun. Secondly, it will enlarge your social support system and professional network. Thirdly, they might be able to help you (and vice versa!), and hence give you a crucial back-up system if things would go awry. Finally, you will normally need multiple references when you apply for jobs after your PhD, so just knowing your supervisor well might not be enough. So, make sure you stay by the coffee machine a few extra minutes to chit-chat. Ask about their day. Help them out. Join the local PhD group (or start one, if needed). You will not regret it.

7. Get praise from elsewhere

Most people need to have a praise/criticism ratio well over one to feel content. However, most PhD supervisors are quite limited in their praise but give their students a lot of criticism. To increase your resilience and happiness, try and increase the praise/criticism ratio by getting praise from other people. It can be your family, friends, or colleagues, but make sure that you have somebody in your corner that tells you "well done!" regularly. Consider teaming up with other students in your group or department/institution and give each other feedback on any first drafts or presentations. Other students should still be able to point out the most important flaws with your work but are usually more inclined to phrase feedback in a positive way. In addition, when you later present the work to your supervisor, it will be more polished and your supervisors are more likely to be pleased with it (or at least less critical).

8. Adhere to all safety and lab routines

You should have been told about any safety regulations when you start, including such simple things as the closest fire exist. You should also have been given thorough instructions on the correct way to handle all chemicals, bacteria, machines, and other things relevant for your lab. If you have not been given such instructions, talk to your supervisor – it is crucial that you and other people are safe.

In addition to safety procedures, make sure that you quickly learn any other routines that are relevant for your lab. How should you name any bacterial strains to be frozen in the communal freezer? What should you do if you use up the last of the antibiotics? Is it okay to use the other lab groups' machines? Some labs may have an actual employed lab manager who you can ask these questions, but in other cases it may be the responsibility of a senior researcher. If there seems to be no agreed-upon lab routines, all chemicals are out of stock, and no machines have been maintained, that is a red flag that maybe you should consider joining another research group instead.

9. Learn any core skills well from the beginning

A lot of skills that you will need in your PhD will have very steep learning curves. It can be tempting to just learn such skills the quick and dirty way, rather than learning them properly. However, the quick and dirty way will often backfire later. For example, if you need to learn to code, just using code from the internet but not understanding how it works will likely take more time in total, instead of taking the time to properly understand it from the start. As another example, if you will be using a wet lab technique, make sure to learn it so well that you get consistent results. Otherwise, you will get a lot of noise and errors in your data and may even have to redo the experiments later. However, do not spend too much time on learning skills that you are not sure that you will be needing. Your PhD project is likely to change dramatically over the years, and you cannot be an expert at everything.

10. Sometimes, you need to do things even if you do not know what you are doing

To a certain extent, a PhD is all about being confused and not knowing what you are doing. It is very common to feel overwhelmed by all the information, methods, and research out there. Some PhD students react by trying to learn everything, at the expense of actually starting to do research.

Naturally, you need to be sure of any research steps where doing them wrong can have severe consequences. However, for a lot of research it is simply a matter of giving it a go, failing, realizing why you failed, change the research protocol, and repeat. In these cases, the fastest way to learn is often to just get started.

11. It is your responsibility to be on top of things

There is a PhD milestone coming up, and you sent the required forms to your supervisors several weeks ago but have not heard anything. What do you do?

You send a polite reminder.

The same thing goes for other deadlines, such as articles where you are first author and conference deadlines. After all, your supervisor likely has a lot of deadlines to keep track on, while you only have a few. Plus, you are much more likely to be negatively impacted by a missed deadline than they are.

12. Do not get stuck

A PhD is about learning how to find information on your own. At the same time, it is very easy to get stuck on something for weeks and weeks, and suddenly you have lost two months on something that could have been resolved quickly if you had reached out for help. In general, if it is something that other people know how to fix, set yourself a deadline for figuring it out on your own and then reach out for help (for possibly unsolvable problems, see the "Projects" section).

Many doctorate students will only ask for help from their supervisors. Sometimes this is a great idea, but do not forget all the other people that you can ask! As mentioned, get to know the people around you and most of them would be happy to help you.

Sometimes you might not know anybody that could help you. In these situations, consider asking other researchers or posting your question online. For me, I think I got a response in about 50% of the cases when I wrote to researchers that I did not know. In my experience, you can increase your success rate of getting responses by:

- Being polite but sincere – it rarely hurts to add a little bit of flattery.

- Being brief yet including all the relevant information.

- Adding "authority" behind your query – for example by cc:ing your supervisor (just check with them first).

- Reference to why you think that they might know the answer to your question, for example if they have written an article about the method that you have a question about.

- Consider e-mailing the less senior person that might know the answer. In my experience, PhD students almost always reply, and they are very likely to help a fellow PhD-student out if they can.

13. Learn how to solve problems

Let us assume that you need to find all the cell types that gene X might be active in, but you have no clue how to find that information and your online searches have been fruitless. Your professor tells you to ask the post-doc in the group. You now have a choice. You can either just ask the post-doc and get a neatly written list with the cell types, or you can ask the post-doc to show you how to find the information.

While the first approach might go quicker the first time, you will not actually have learned how to solve the problem. If you learn how to do it yourself, you will know how to find the answer for all similar questions in the future. Some of the most useful skills that you can learn is how to find information and solve problems.

14. See the first quarter of your PhD as learning time

It is easy to feel disheartened (or panicked) a year or two into your PhD if you have not managed to make significant progress on your thesis. However, there is a lot to learn to be able to produce high-quality research. Many doctorate students do not produce any material that are included in their theses until their final years. Therefore, see the first quarter or so of your PhD as learning time and do not panic if you have not produced anything that can be included in your thesis by the end of that period.

However, if you have not produced anything *and* do not have a clear idea on how you will achieve something tangible for the next quarter of your program, then it is time to strongly consider making some drastic changes. In these cases, you need to carefully evaluate your situation to decide on the best course of action (see the section "Figuring out what the problem is").

15. Objectively evaluate your progress regularly

There will be periods in your PhD where everything is going splendidly and you make rapid progress, and then there will be long periods where it feels like everything is failing. I would highly recommend that you regularly sit down and objectively evaluate your progress. Do not evaluate how you feel that it is going but look at what you have objectively accomplished relative to your end goal (your thesis) as well as your current trajectory.

Every three months or so, I suggest that you list all your achievements to date and compare them to your end goal (fulfilling your graduation requirements). For example, you might have completed 50% of the mandatory coursework, have one article out under review, and have completed an estimated 50% of your next article. If you need three articles to graduate, you are about 50% through – how does that compare to how far along your program you are? However, remember that the first quarter of your PhD is usually spent on learning the basics, so do not panic if you have done a bit more than 50% of your PhD. However, if you are in the final year of your PhD and have only completed 50% of what is needed for your thesis, you need to actively think through what you are going to do. Can you switch to more low-risk, low-reward projects so that you can finish on time? Can you extend your PhD? Can you bulk up some of your other thesis chapters with a few more sensitivity analyses, and have fewer thesis chapters instead? Think through your options and talk to your supervisor. By evaluating your progress regularly, you will catch any problems while there is still time to make larger changes so that you can graduate on time.

Similarly, it is a good idea to evaluate your current "trajectory" every few weeks. That is, rather than just evaluating how the current week has gone, look back at the last couple of weeks and judge if you have been moving in the right direction on average. Have you spent your time on things that actually matter for your thesis? If you have learned new skills, was it worth learning them? It is very easy to get caught up in "side-quests" as a PhD student, where you can spend many months on research projects, analyses, or courses that are irrelevant for your thesis. While part of a PhD is supposed to be detours – that is how you learn – spotting meaningless detours early on is key to having a PhD with reasonable working hours and graduating on time.

16. Remember that things might not be possible

In school, all problems are solvable and the amount of work you are given are always possible to finish in the time allocated. This is not the case in a PhD. Projects *may not be possible to do,* and *they might not be doable in the allotted time.*

17. Emotionally judge your performance based on time put in

It is very difficult to judge how far along a PhD you are, and it is very easy to feel like you are not getting anything done. It is also easy to compare yourself with your most successful colleagues and feel like a failure, regardless of how well you are actually doing (for more information about this, see the section "Impostor syndrome").

However, every PhD project is different. Some will be lucky and have a very easy one. Some will end up with projects where one thing after another goes wrong for years. Hence, I strongly recommend that you start to "emotionally" judge your performance based on the time and effort you have spent rather than actual results. Instead of feeling like a failure because the week's experiments failed, ask yourself if you worked dedicatedly the 40 hours that you had set out to do this week (or whatever goal you had). If you worked dedicatedly those hours, think of the week as a success.

One thought that also helped me was to think that 50% of the work I do in my PhD will not amount to anything. In hindsight, that proportion was probably closer to 80%. I then considered that 50% (or 80%) of "wasted" time to be part of what I had to do in my PhD. Whenever I had a week with zero progress, I "budgeted" it to the 50% of work that I "knew" was going to be wasted, and then I felt better.

Courses

Some departments/institutions and universities require you to take a set number of courses, others do not require their PhD students to do any. In general, consider either spreading the courses out evenly during your PhD for timely breaks or completing them early in your PhD to have them out of the way. However, I would recommend that you avoid scheduling any mandatory courses in the end of your PhD when you are usually most productive in your research. In addition, if the courses are useful, it is better to learn the material earlier in your PhD.

Your time is valuable. Only sign up for courses that are 1) mandatory, 2) useful, or 3) fun. As a new PhD student, it can be easy to sign up to a lot of "technical" courses that are only slightly related to your field. You are not expected to know everything tangentially related to your field, so spending too much time learning skills you do not need is inefficient.

Similarly, since course quality can vary, you may want to talk to other students or read some course reviews before you sign up for a course, so that your time is not wasted. In hindsight, the courses I am most happy about having taken were the ones for transferrable skills, such as writing, presenting, and making figures. In these courses, I learned things that will be useful regardless of what I do for the rest of my career, and they were also a fun break from the daily routines. Besides courses that are offered by universities, there are many online courses and resources available, for example through Coursera, Khan Academy, and YouTube. Many scientific institutions and companies also share videos online that explain complicated concepts and procedures. Large conferences may also upload talks and lectures after the conference, which can be a great activity for days when you are running low on motivation.

Finally, consider what courses might advance your post-PhD career. If you already know what jobs you want afterwards, it might be smart to target your courses to those jobs. For example, if you would like to do a career in scientific writing and publishing after your PhD, you might want to prioritize writing courses over technical courses.

Research projects

As explained in the "What is a PhD?" section, doctorate program structures can vary considerable between different fields. This section is directed to students whose PhDs will consist of several smaller research projects. Usually, if you are doing such a program, your overarching PhD project sets the rough scope of your thesis, but the individual research projects will then make up the thesis chapters. While your overarching PhD topic is usually quite fixed, there is often some flexibility in deciding what research projects to work on throughout your doctorate journey. You will usually decide on what research project to do next together with your supervisor, and it is common that the original plan for what projects you will do changes dramatically over the course of your PhD. However, how much flexibility you have is dependent on your supervisor – some supervisors are not open to discuss what research projects their students should work on.

Getting good research projects is fundamental for having a nice and easy PhD journey. But what is a good research project and how do you get them? While this differs between fields, I recommend that you try and estimate the reward/cost ratio for potential projects before you spend too much time on them:

1. What are the estimated rewards of this research project?

Consider if the suggested project is helping you towards your end goal – getting that PhD. Will you be able to include it in your thesis? If not, will you learn important skills that will bring you closer to your goal? If not, is it likely to give you a publication or put you in good favor with your supervisor? Make sure that at least some of the projects that you work on can be included in your thesis. You only have a set number of years of funding, and almost all projects take longer than you expect. It may help to try and figure out what your supervisor's aim with the project is. Is your supervisor thinking that there is a 1% chance that you discover something revolutionary, but that the project most likely will not be publishable at all? Is the project for you to learn a certain skill? Is the project to be published, regardless of the results? Is the project just to satiate your supervisor's curiosity? Knowing your supervisor's reason for assigning you the project should aid you in determining the estimated reward for you.

The criteria for whether a project can be included in your thesis or not vary between universities and departments/institutions. However, if you are at a department/institution where a thesis must consist of a number of published articles, you might want to try and avoid being put on research projects that your supervisor is not planning to publish. For example, while it might be nice of you to do a pilot study for your supervisor's grant application, it may not always be in your best interest to spend time on it. If you are at a department/institution where all of your thesis chapters need to pertain to a specific subject, you may also want to avoid accepting research projects that span too many different areas. In addition, remember that the research projects that you include in your thesis need to be of sufficiently high quality for you to successfully defend them at your final thesis defense. Therefore, you do not want to spend too much time on research projects that have fundamental, unresolved flaws, such as too small sample sizes or major methodological issues.

Finally, also consider the risk of being scooped. Being scooped means that some other research group publishes an almost identical project before you do. Depending on your thesis requirements, this could mean that an entire research project suddenly cannot be published as an article or included in your thesis. While it seems quite rare to be completely scooped (that is, that you cannot publish the project at all), it is something to keep in mind.

2. What are the estimated costs of this research project?

Before you embark on a research project, consider what it would require in terms of data, money, skills, time, and quality of life. For example, what data would you need for the project? Is the data already publicly available, available from another research group, or would you have to generate it yourself? Would you have to do field work in a remote part of the Siberian tundra for three years? How long would it take to generate or obtain the data? If your research involves humans or animals, generating data can also be lined with costly ethical and legal hurdles that could take many months or even years to overcome.

Similarly, what skills would this research project require? Learning new skills take time, especially if there is nobody else in your group that can teach you. If you do not have the skills that you would need for the research project, how long would it take for you to learn them?

Finally, what will it cost in terms of time? For this consideration, do not trust your supervisor's word on how long it will take. It would not be uncommon for a supervisor to estimate that something will take a month and it then ends up taking a year. It is easy to only think about the main analyses before you begin a project. However, as time goes on you often notice mistakes that you need to fix or realize that you need to do several sensitivity analyses before you can trust your results. Quite often, even though the actual experiments might not take too much time to do, it may take considerable time for you to learn how to do the experiments or the analyses properly. In addition, if the project is to be published it generally takes a lot of time to write the article and go through the review process (see the "Publishing" section). For me, it seemed that most research projects took three times longer than most people thought in the beginning, but I am sure this can differ a lot.

In summary, try and estimate the rewards and the costs of a research project before you start, as it will allow you to choose projects with a high estimated reward/cost ratio. An ideal research project is a project that is easy, goes relatively quick, and only uses data and skills that you already have, can easily attain, or want to learn. Ideally, it is publishable *regardless* of the results, is strongly related to your thesis topic, and will be possible to include in your thesis no matter what.

So, how do you get such a project?

First of all, I would highly recommend that you literally ask for a simple and straightforward project as your first research project. For example, perhaps you could just replicate the findings from a study using a different dataset or do a small part of a more experienced colleague's research project. You usually do not have the expertise to judge how feasible a research project is in the beginning of your PhD, and with the above suggestions you will either just need to follow the methods section in the original paper or ask your senior colleague if you run into problems. If these options are not possible and it is difficult to estimate the reward/cost ratio, consider simply starting on the new research project and see how far you have gotten after six to eight weeks. By then, you should have a much better idea of how feasible the research project is and if it is worth spending more time on.

In general, do not blindly accept all the projects that your supervisor wants you to work on. If your supervisor wants you to work on a bad research project, you may be able to decline. Some supervisors get upset if students refuse to work on a project, so you may want to consider alternative strategies than a downright "no". Can you negotiate with your supervisor? Can you agree to spend a certain amount of time on it? With some supervisors, the best strategy might even be to say that you will do it and then just work on the projects that you prefer until your supervisor forgets about it, even if it feels unprofessional.

When you have become more experienced in your field, you may be able to avoid bad research projects by suggesting good research projects yourself. Spend some time trying to come up with projects that fit the criteria, and then either just start working on them or ask your supervisor if you can work on them – the best strategy depends on your supervisor. Spend some time thinking about how you will present the idea. In general, it is advisable to stress how the research project might find very interesting results rather than that it will be easy for you. Think through what excites your supervisor and emphasize those parts of the suggested project. In addition, suggesting your own projects have the added benefits that you can choose which skills to learn, and you seem like a very ambitious student.

Some supervisors tend to add more and more research projects to their PhD students' to-do lists, and rarely remove any. In fact, it is not uncommon for supervisors to even forget what they have previously asked their students to do, and projects that they were very excited about a few months ago are suddenly considered boring. Hence, make sure that you are in control of your to-do list and that you work on things that are worth your time and energy. Personally, I would recommend not working on more than two research projects at the same time. It takes time to switch between projects, and rather than working on four research projects for four years, it is more satisfying to work on one project each year and then be completely finished with it. Finishing projects early in your PhD will give you a sense of satisfaction, and results in fewer things on your to-do list at any one time. It also translates into a lower risk of getting scooped as your early projects will be published quicker and you can alter any remaining projects that you have planned to do if somebody publishes something similar.

Finally, try to finish projects that could be included in your thesis with a little bit of extra work. Six half-done great projects are often more difficult to make into a thesis than three finalized okay projects. Still, remember that some projects may be impossible or cost too much to complete. In these cases, the smartest thing may be to give the project up as early as you can. The worst-case scenario is not a project failing, but a project that fails after you have spent years on it.

Managing your supervisory relationship

So, you have hopefully found a good supervisor (or supervisors) for you and your project. How do you best utilize your supervisor's time and effort, and minimize the risks of problems between you and your supervisor? Below, I have outlined some key advice. However, if you find that you are experiencing problems in your supervisory relationship, I recommend that you read through the section "Problems with your supervisor" as well.

1. Understand that you and your supervisor's interests may be in conflict with each other

The primary aim for most supervisors is to publish a lot of high-impact papers, preferentially with as little work as possible for them. However, most doctorate students would say that their primary aim is to graduate on time. It is important that you recognize that you and your supervisor's interests may not align, as it may explain the rationale behind your supervisor's decisions and actions (thank you to Dr. Nick Crang for teaching me this). In addition, different end goals are also a common source of conflict between a student and a supervisor.

2. Make sure that you are all on the same page

Often, your PhD project will not be fully outlined when you start your PhD, but rather a vaguely expressed project aim. If you have several supervisors, they may also have very different ideas of what your actual research projects should be about, what datasets you should work on, who you should collaborate with, etc. I highly recommend that you try to get all your supervisors together to discuss exactly what your first research project should be in detail and have a rough sketch of what your other research projects should be. In addition to deciding on what research projects you should do, also make sure that you agree on any practical aspects (such as which research group you should sit in). It is crucial that your supervisors can reach agreements about you and your projects so that you do not lose valuable time and spend your PhD being torn in different directions. If your supervisors cannot reach a basic agreement on your first research project in the first month or two, you should see it as a potential red flag and consider making changes in your supervisory arrangement. Even if you only have one supervisor, you should make sure that the two of you can agree on the basic practicalities of your project within the first month or two. If your supervisor is very vague, ignores you, or cannot make decisions, that is another red flag that you need to make some changes.

What changes you need to make depends completely on the situation. In some cases, it may be enough to change how you interact with your supervisor. For example, you may need to become more active in booking meetings, setting agendas, and asking for help. If the problem is that your two supervisors cannot get along, perhaps you need to choose one supervisor over the other. Unfortunately, there is no one-solution-fit-all for these circumstances. Therefore, carefully consider your options and do not hesitate to confidentially talk to any student representatives or any professor responsible for student welfare at your department.

3. Set up regular supervisory meetings

Unless you have a supervisor that is very hands-on, you should consider setting up regular supervisory meetings. How often you should have supervisory meetings depends on your field, department/institution, and other things, but in general I would say at least once every fortnight. Having regular supervisory meetings will minimize the risk of being stuck for prolonged periods of time.

4. Think things through before your supervisory meetings

Try and figure out what you want out of the meeting before the actual meeting, and think through how to respond to potential questions, suggestions, and criticism from your supervisors. If you want to get permission to run certain analyses, consider listing arguments in favor of doing them. If you want to drop a certain project, carefully think through all your arguments beforehand. If you are stuck, think through potential solutions so that you can present them to your supervisor. Knowing what you want out of the meeting will help you prepare for the meeting and maximize your chances of getting what you need to succeed.

5. Prepare for your supervisory meetings

Senior academics are usually very busy. Hence, prepare for your supervisory meetings by sending out an agenda beforehand. Consider preparing slides or bullet points with what you have done since the last meeting and list any major questions that needs to be answered or decisions that needs to be made. Remember that supervisors are often involved in many different projects and that they may not remember the specifics about your project, so consider giving them a quick summary in the beginning of the meeting. In addition, preparing a summary has the added benefit of collecting your own thoughts about the project.

6. Show your supervisors results and figures

All supervisors are different, but it seems like they all love to see tangible results. Showing what you have done since the last supervisory

44

meeting with a results figure makes your progress more tangible. Remember that you can also make figures and flowcharts of your methods, which may be easier to follow than dense text. If you can, consider making the figures good enough to include in your thesis to save time later.

7. Make sure that you understand what your supervisors are saying

It is very common for supervisors to overestimate how much doctorate students know when they start their PhD. Your supervisors will commonly have worked in the field for many years or even decades, and a lot of things seem obvious to them. While you will likely have to accept a certain degree of confusion, ask for clarifications for all the things that you cannot look up yourself after the supervisory meeting. Is your supervisor talking about research by somebody called "Löfwenström-Viedermann" that you realize at once you will have no idea how to spell or find the author's publications later? Ask them to write down the name. Is your supervisor telling you to do something, but there are five different methods to do it? Ask if they have any preference which method you should use or if they would like you to read up about all the methods and evaluate them. Do they want an analysis to be quick and dirty, or is it something that should be publishable? Ask questions until you have a basic understanding of what you need to do and how to get started. However, also try and avoid irritating your supervisors by asking too many questions. Sometimes, you can also go to other members in your research group and ask. Perhaps "Löfwenström-Viedermann" is the most well-known researcher in the field, and your fellow PhD colleagues can help you with the spelling.

8. Consider sending summaries out after every supervisory meeting

Sending out a summary after each supervisory meeting will make sure that you are all on the same page and may be highly useful in case of any future disagreements about what was said.

9. Do not ask questions that an online search could answer

Both your supervisor's time and your colleagues' time are valuable. Do not ask them questions that an online search could answer in a reasonable time – it can really irritate people. One of the most important skills to learn as a PhD student is how to find information.

10. Your supervisors do not know everything

It is easy to think that your supervisor knows all the nitty-gritty details about everything in your field, sort of like an all-knowing encyclopedia. Unfortunately, this is rarely the case, and it is not uncommon for your supervisor to never have used the machine that you are wondering what settings to use for. In addition, many professors do not like to be asked detailed questions about things that they think are minor details. On the other hand, some other member in your group may be using the machine daily. Therefore, actively think about which group member is best suited to answer your question rather than automatically asking your supervisor.

11. You are (most likely) less important to your supervisor than they are to you

Many PhD students worry about what their supervisors think of them. To seem competent, PhD students can spend an hour writing their supervisors an e-mail and spend the entire weekend finalizing the last experiments before their next supervisory meeting. Quite often, the only response to the painfully written e-mail will be "ok" and the supervisor will cancel the meeting in the last minute.

These situations stem from the fact that the doctorate student is, usually, a whole lot less important to their supervisor than vice versa. Most PhD students need their supervisors, both in their daily life and to get good references for the future. The supervisors do not need each individual doctorate student in the same way, and they normally have a lot of other claims on their time. So, if you feel a bit ignored, do not worry about it if you are still getting the help that you need. It is just part of the life of a PhD student.

12. Your supervisors are human

It might not feel that way, but your supervisors are human. A few personal touches, like remembering their kids' names and asking about them, can go a long way in making your supervisor positively inclined towards you. Also, remember that things that go on in their personal life may affect their mood, just like it can for everybody else. Do not assume that your supervisor's irritability is because of you when it might be that they are in the middle of a divorce.

Similarly – supervisors can be wrong. When students start their PhD, it is very common to think that supervisors know how to solve all problems, and that they even know what the results will be. This is not the case! Supervisors are only human, and although they should know more about your PhD project in the beginning, this will change quickly. Many professors are very good at giving an all-knowing impression, even when they might not know what they are talking about. Hence, listen to your supervisors, but remember to double-check crucial information or anything that does not make sense.

13. Actively try and figure out how your supervisor's mind works

Supervisors have different preferences. Some tend to get started on lengthy discussions about methods, others will only want to talk about results. Some prefer meetings, others prefer to respond over e-mail. Some will generate lots of grand ideas every meeting, others will want everything to be perfect with your current analyses before moving on to the next step.

You may be lucky and have a perfect fit with your supervisor, but usually there will be at least some minor differences in how you work. I would encourage you to actively try and figure out if and where you differ, and how to manage the differences. Sometimes it might be possible to talk about it. For example, perhaps your supervisor comes up with ten new grand ideas that you could do every supervisory meeting, which stresses you out because you perceive the ideas as "do these things as well". In such a case, if you talk to your supervisor, they might be very surprised and tell you that it was just ideas, not orders of what to do. Similarly, if your supervisor rarely gives praise, consider changing your "internal supervisor dictionary" so that an "okay" from your supervisor means "well done!".

14. Learn how to handle disagreements with your supervisor

Sooner or later, you will disagree with your supervisor about something. How you should deal with this depends on what the issue is, your supervisor's personality, and how your relationship with your supervisor is.

When you have a disagreement with your supervisor, carefully analyze the situation and make sure that you understand your supervisor's point

47

of view. What are the pros and cons with both you and your supervisor's suggestion? Is it just different ways of doing something, or do you think that your supervisor's suggestion would be objectively wrong? If it takes more time to do it your supervisor's way, will it perhaps be more robust?

In general, you want to avoid antagonizing your supervisor. While scientific disagreements can teach both you and your supervisor a lot, try and keep them light-hearted so that your relationship is not damaged. Unless you think that your supervisor's suggestion would be objectively wrong and might damage your research, it may be wisest to just go with your supervisor's suggestion if they have made up their mind. If you think that they are objectively wrong and that doing as your supervisor says might have consequences, perhaps you can suggest talking to some other senior researchers about it or doing it both ways and compare? Or perhaps you could send your supervisor some articles that demonstrate why your suggestion is better?

Back things up

It is absolutely crucial that you back up your data, code, results, figures, thesis drafts, and other things safely and regularly, ideally in two separate locations. Do not assume that the university servers are automatically backed up without knowing. When you back-up things, make sure that you conform to any regulations about data security, privacy, etc.

Consider possible worst-case scenarios, like a fire in your department or a thief stealing your computer. How much work would be lost? Do not put yourself in a position where you will have to redo months or years of work because you did not back up your data.

Language

You need to be able to communicate with your supervisor, your research group, the rest of the academic world, as well as potentially with the local people where you are doing your PhD. Many research groups communicate in English, but your research group's main communication language may also be the local language or whichever language the majority of the group members speak. You also need to be able to communicate with the rest of the research world – which usually means mastering reading and writing in English. Consider improving your language skills even if you are a native English speaker. Being a native speaker is not a guarantee that you can produce academic texts of sufficiently high quality.

The sooner that you get proficient at English (and any other necessary language), the better. If you can, consider taking language courses even before you start your PhD. Many universities offer free academic English courses for their students. Another good tip is to try and immerse yourself in the language, for example by watching videos and reading books in the language. Many e-readers and e-book software have dictionaries that you can install, so that you only have to click on a word to get a translation. Consider having online language exchanges with native English speakers that want to learn your language. You can usually find such people by asking in expatriate groups for your home country on social media. It is also great if you can make friends that speak the language that you have to practice. To learn more rapidly, do your best to speak even if you feel like you are making mistakes. If needed and allowed, you can also consider hiring an English proof-reader before submitting articles or theses (sometimes such costs can be taken from your scholarship).

Reading scientific articles

You will read a lot of scientific articles during your PhD. I read about 500 articles and skimmed through about 500 articles during my time as a graduate student. I have no idea how many thousands abstracts I read.

Learning how to read an article quickly will be very well spent time. Researchers have different preferences, and the best way to approach an article also depends on your field and what you want out of the article.

Personally, I always start with reading the abstract in detail. After that, I decide whether it is worth my time to read the rest. When I first started my PhD, I always read the introduction in detail after that, so that I could understand the rest of the paper. However, as I became more knowledgeable in my field, I started to just skim through the introduction quickly or even skipped it at first.

With time, I also learned to target my reading to what I wanted out of it. If I wanted to learn more about how to apply a method, I read the methods section in detail. If I wanted to see if a paper contained a certain piece of information that I needed a reference for, I focused on the results or just searched for key words. The discussion section was very helpful in the beginning of my PhD to learn about the strengths and limitations of different methods and/or studies, but with time I focused less on the discussion. However, some researchers use completely different methods to approach articles, for example looking at the figures first.

The main point is – do not just read a paper in detail from start to finish. Reading all potentially relevant papers in detail takes too much time. Instead, think about what you want out of the paper. Do you need to find a reference for something that you already know is true? Do you want to learn more about how to use a specific method? Do you want to learn more about the field in general? Do you want ideas on how to make figures to show your own results?

I would also strongly recommend that you create a system to organize the articles that you have read and plan to read. Even such a thing as what to name a saved article is not straightforward. Calling articles by their title can be confusing, especially as senior academics tend to refer to papers as "that paper by Smith in *The Best Scientific Journal Ever*" rather than the title – where Smith tends to be one of the senior/last authors on the paper rather than the first author. In many fields, the more junior researchers who did the actual work are placed first in the author list, and the more senior researchers who generated ideas, funding, etc., are placed last. In fields with this system, it is more prestigious to be the first or the last author than a middle author.

The system that I started using after a while was "First author last name" "Last author last name" "Year of publication" "–", "title". For example, an article could be called "Andersson Smith 2020 – Sieving biases in a colander-based system". That system worked very well for me, as I then automatically learned the senior author on each article, which helped when I wanted to talk to colleagues about a paper. I also got a rough idea of when each article had been written, which helped me establish a mental timeline of how the field had changed over the years. In hindsight, it would have been good to also include the abbreviated journal name, as senior colleagues often just referred to articles as "that recent paper about sieving biases in *The Best Scientific Journal Ever*".

Sometimes, I wrote a brief description of the key findings or if they had used certain methods settings that I might need to reference later in my research journal. In hindsight, I wish I would have done this from the start in some sort of spreadsheet or document with added key words, or perhaps have used the more advanced features offered by reference managers. In summary, make sure that you have a good system for reading and saving articles, and for retrieving key information from them.

Writing and proofreading

You will need to write and proofread a lot of things before, during, and after your PhD, including your program application, papers, e-mails, data access forms, ethics applications, your thesis, and much more. Writing skills is something that you can improve, just like all other skills, and I would highly recommend you to take a writing course. However, below I have added some specific tips and tricks that I picked up during my PhD:

1. Choose word processor and reference manager wisely

All word processors have different pros and cons. Some have highly specialized tools for complex formatting, others cannot make a single page into landscape format and keep the rest as portrait format. Some offer features where several people can edit a document online at the same time, for others you will need to send the document back and forth between authors. Some have great track-changes features, others are limited. Some are great for making mathematic functions, others cannot handle functions at all.

Different word processors are also compatible with different reference managers. Reference managers can be used to save any articles and to properly cite them as needed. Choose one early on in your PhD, and I would recommend considering going with the same one as your supervisor (or whoever it is that you will ping articles and your thesis back and forth with). Make sure that you consistently add articles that you might reference to the system. However, do not trust the reference manager – it is very common that articles are saved incorrectly, so look them over as you go to save time in the future. Different reference managers also have different strengths and limitations, but a key thing to check is that it can handle hundreds of references – you do not want it to crash while you are finalizing your thesis.

The features of different word processors and reference managers change regularly, hence I have not compared them here. However, for word processors you may want to check out Microsoft Word, Pages, Google Docs, LaTeX, or LibreOffice, and for reference managers Mendeley, EndNote, Zotero, and Paperpile. Some of these resources are, at the time of writing, free to use, and others you may be able to get for free through your university. Consider what you need and prefer for your specific project, try out several options and make sure that your choice is compatible with the people you collaborate with. Although you can export text from one word processor to another, it often messes up formatting and references, which can drive both you and your collaborators crazy.

2. Use the formatting settings

Most commonly used word processors have various tools to help you format your document. For example, you can assign headers on different levels, and then for example say that all headers on level 1 should always start on a new page or be a certain font size. I highly recommend learning these tools for the word processor that you use, as it will save you a lot of time in the long run. You *do not* want to manually create a table of contents for your thesis.

3. Stick to either American or British English

For non-native English speakers, it is easy to switch back and forth between American and British English when you write. While this might seem like a minor issue, it can be irritating for native speakers so choose which one to use depending on your target audience. For example, if you are at a British university, you may need to use British spelling, and vice versa. Some journals may specify whether articles should be in British or American English. Remember that you can change the language settings in most word processors so that it will highlight misspelled words.

4. Make it easy for the reader

When starting in academia, it is easy to think that articles should be difficult to read, as they often are. Yet, everybody appreciates an easy-to-read article. Here are some concrete tips on how to make a text easier to read:

- Use active rather than passive voice. It is easier to read sentences that are structured as "we cultivated the cells in medium for 30 minutes" (active voice) than "the cells were cultivated in medium for 30 minutes" (passive voice).

- Opt for shorter sentences rather than longer. As a rule of thumb, make sure that all sentences are shorter than three rows.

- Vary the sentence length and sentence structure to make the text more interesting to read.

- Only have one or two distinct pieces of information in a single sentence.

- Use simple, yet specific, words.

- When listing things in a sentence, start with the shortest word and end with the longest. For example, if you want to list colors, list them as red, blue, green, and orange. That order flows easier for the reader than orange, green, blue, and red.

- Use as few abbreviations as possible, and if you use abbreviations, opt for the ones commonly used in your field rather than making up new ones.

- Transition words are words like however, but, therefore, consequently, similarly, etc. When you use transition words, you prepare the reader for what will come next, which will make the text easier to read.

- Avoid negatives such as "not". For example, instead of writing "do not use negatives", you can write "avoid negatives" to make your writing easier to follow.

- Plan your writing. What are you going to talk about in each paragraph? Each paragraph should concern a distinct idea in your paper or thesis. If you do not know what information you want to convey in a paragraph, it will not be clear for the reader either. Headings and subheadings are great for making a piece of text easier to both write and read. Sometimes, I would even add headings first, so that the purpose of the paragraph became clear to me, and then remove them after I have finished the text.

- Put the most important things in a paragraph or a paper first or last. Readers remember the things at the end of a paragraph best, then the things in the beginning the second best, and tend to forget the middle part.

- End complicated paragraphs with a conclusion sentence and end complicated documents with a conclusion paragraph.

Something that helped me a lot was to go over a shorter piece of text multiple times. I would then focus on of these issues each time I went over the text, which tended to really improve the text.

5. Write and complete things well ahead of any deadlines

Writing things with time to spare will mean higher quality and less stress. It also allows for better proofreading, as described in the next point.

6. Take breaks in the writing process

Taking a few breaks between writing and proofreading will allow you to look at your writing with fresh eyes. Your brain will actually read what you have written rather than remember what you wanted to say, and it will then be a lot easier to spot any mistakes or incoherencies.

7. Read it over multiple times, and look for different things each time

It is difficult to proofread for scientific accuracy, grammar, spelling, formatting, sentence structure, figure and table referencing, and article references at the same time. I highly advise looking over your writing focusing on one issue each time.

8. Use the search function

The search and replace function is invaluable. For example, if you are checking that all the references to the tables are correct, just search for "table" and in most cases you will want the reference to the table and the table to come after each other. Are there any words that you tend to misspell, or do you tend to mix up "there" and "their"? Search for them, and remember that you can search for parts of words as well.

9. Change font when proofreading and/or listen to your text

One of the best tips I have ever gotten for proofreading is to change the font from serif to sans-serif, or vice versa, when it is time to proofread. Basically, it makes your brain see your writing as a new text and makes it much easier to spot any errors and get a feeling for how the text flows. So, when it becomes time to proofread, change the font to one that looks completely different. Similarly, it might be useful to use the automatic reading tools that read the text back to you, so that you can listen to your text rather than read it.

10. If you are dyslectic, consider using a font made for dyslectics

Nowadays, there are fonts that are specifically made for people with dyslexia that makes the text easier to read.

11. Compare documents feature

Some word processors have a tool where you can compare two documents, and any chances will be highlighted. This can be a very useful tool if you need to be sure what changes have been made between two documents, for example if your supervisor has forgotten to use track-changes.

12. Get feedback from others

Getting your writing back covered in red can feel like a failure. Yet, getting criticism is the best way to learn and improve. When it comes to getting feedback on your writing, try and get as specific feedback as possible. For example, if a sentence is difficult to understand, what exactly is it that makes it difficult to understand? Is it because of poor grammar or incorrect use of words? Is it that the sentence is too long? Does the sentence introduce too many new ideas? Are you going into too much detail or too little detail? For complicated concepts or methods, maybe a figure would make things easier for the reader?

When you go over the feedback, try and understand the feedback rather than just doing as the proof-reader says. For example, if the proof-reader has changed "the data is" to "the data are", look up why your first suggestion was wrong (in this case, the word "data" is plural form, and it should therefore be written as "the data are"). This way, you can avoid making the same writing mistakes over and over again.

13. Consider using a writing assistant and plagiarism checks

Writing assistants, whether included in your word processors or online tools such as Grammarly, may help you spot more mistakes as well as improve the flow of your writing. While some of them may cost money, it may be worth paying some money to decrease the number of times you have to send your writing back-and-forth to your supervisor. In addition, some online tools can also check for plagiarism, which can easily happen if you have just accidentally forgotten that you copy/pasted something from an article. However, before submitting your writing anywhere, make sure that it is not a scam – there has been cases where "companies" have resold academic texts to students wanting essays.

Figures

Many students will need to produce figures during their PhD, such as flowcharts to illustrate the methods or figures that present the results. Still, a lot of researchers never learn how to make good figures, even though there are many good reasons to learn it:

- Figures may convey difficult concepts better than text.

- They can convey large-scale results in a more intuitive way than a table.

- They tend to be less daunting for readers than text.

- They can help reduce your word count, which is often a limiting factor when writing articles and theses.

- They can make your article or presentation seem more professional.

- Many researchers start "reading" any article with looking at the figures, and thereafter decide whether to read the article or not.

- A lot of supervisors prefer to see figures over text.

- If you are good at making figures, your supervisor may involve you in more projects, leading to more publications on your part.

In hindsight, my PhD would have been a lot easier if I would have spent a couple of weeks learning how to make good figures in the beginning. Since I did not learn the skill properly at first, making good figures took a lot of time. I was therefore hesitant about making figures for my supervisory meetings and usually presented my results at supervisory meetings in tables or bullet points instead, which caused my supervisory meetings to be less efficient. All in all, it would have been time well spent to learn to do it properly.

So, how do you make good figures?

1. Figure out what software is best for producing the kind of figures that you will need

Usually, there will be some "go-to" plotting software that are used in your research group and/or field. My recommendation is to talk to older colleagues and find out which ones they are using and why. However, learning one software may not be enough. One software might be great for plotting results, but another one much better for making methods flowcharts or to integrate photos.

If you are likely to have to produce a lot of figures during your PhD, I would strongly recommend you to take a data visualization course where you learn a professional illustrating software, such as Inkscape, Adobe Illustrator, or Affinity Designer. While professional software usually has a steeper learning curve, the end results are usually a lot prettier and looks more professional.

2. Take a course in the software of your choice

There are a lot of courses where you can learn how to make good figures. For most software, there will be good, free online courses and video tutorials on Youtube.

3. Look at figures presenting similar data/concepts in other articles

It is inefficient to re-invent the wheel, so look at how other people have presented similar information before you get started on your figure. If you have used a common method and dataset, chances are there will be figures out there presenting similar data in different ways. Take a critical look at the figures that you find to decide how you can optimize your own figure.

Remember that you do not actually need to read through all the articles for this step. Sometimes, you can just search for the method name or the kind of plot that you want to make and see what image results comes up.

4. Start with sketching on paper

Before you make a complicated figure, think it through by drawing different ideas using pen and paper. What should the axes be? Where should different text boxes be? Should a flowchart be horizontal or vertical? How should you make the distinctions between different study groups? How should you indicate intervention? Drawing ideas on paper first will save you time in the long run, since it is a lot quicker than making a real figure on the computer.

5. Follow the standards in your field

Usually, there will be some standards in your field, such as certain ways to indicate wild type versus mutant, if axes are exponential or not, etc. It is usually best to follow these standards as much as you can so that the readers do not get confused.

If you do not want to follow the "standards", make sure that your choices are not confusing. For example, I did not want to color code men with blue and women with pink as it felt too stereotypical for me. However, it would have been very confusing for the reader if I would have coded women blue and men pink. Hence, I used different colors to code for sex.

6. Check the author guidelines (or similar) before you start

If you are making a figure for an article, there will likely be restrictions regarding figure size, font type, font size, etc. You can save yourself a lot of work by looking at these requirements on the journal webpage before you start the actual plotting. If you and your supervisor have not decided on which journal to submit to yet, you could just look at the most likely ones and try and make a figure that roughly adheres to all the journals' guidelines.

Similarly, if you will have to rewrite your articles into a thesis, I strongly recommend making two versions of each figure when you are wrapping up a research project. One figure that follows the journal requirements, and one figure that follows your thesis formatting requirements (information about your local thesis formatting requirements should be available through your department/institution). If you plot figures with a consistent layout from the start, you will save yourself a lot of time at the end of your PhD.

7. Always save your code and raw figures that may be needed later in a safe and organized way

You are very likely to have to return to figures years after you originally made them. For example, you may realize that you need to change the font size for a figure you made your first year for your thesis. In most cases, you will not remember what you called it or how you made it years later. Therefore, always make sure that you save any code or files that have been used to generate figures in an organized and safe way. As a good rule of thumb, you should have organized it in such a way that a stranger in your field could redo the figure from your documentation.

8. Do not mislead readers

Null results are okay. Misleading figures are not. Hence, be very careful that your images do not mislead the readers. For example, if your axis should start at 0, you either start it at 0 or make it extremely clear that it is not.

9. Choose colors and layout wisely

Many people are colorblind. Any potential reviewers or assessors that are colorblind will not be happy if they cannot understand your figures. Similarly, it is common for potential reviewers and assessors to print out articles and theses in black and white. For these reasons, try and make your study groups distinct in more ways than color. For example, you could have different patterns on your bars, label them, or have different dash types. In addition, you can use websites such as Colorbrewer (https://colorbrewer2.org/), where you can find nice-looking color schemes that fit different criteria.

10. Make it easy for the reader

Try and see your figure from a novel perspective. Is everything intuitive? For example, if you are having differently dashed lines represent different groups, where have you put the label? A reader will have to think a lot more if the labels for the dashes are in a separate box, compared to if the labels are right next to the line on the plot.

11. Get feedback

Ask other people in your group, other PhD students, or family and friends about what they think is good and bad with your figures (or at least some of them). It is very difficult to see your figures as other people see them.

12. Have fun!

Making figures was my absolute favorite thing to do in my PhD. It is a chance to be creative and have fun – so put on some good music and have fun!

Publishing papers

One of the first things you should have in mind when contributing to a paper is the author list, especially if your thesis will be article-based. Technically, the author list is only supposed to include people that have contributed substantially to a paper, but how much a person needs to contribute to be included differs vastly between fields and supervisors. In some cases, only the people who have generated and analyzed a substantial part of the data will be included. In other cases, several of the authors on a paper will have done very little or next to nothing. Your supervisors might ask that authors are added because of political reasons, as a "thank you" for having sent an e-mail to a third party, or just for having been present in a meeting.

How you list authors also differ between fields and journals. In some fields, it is common that the first author in the list is the junior author (the one who did most of the actual work), and the last (or senior) author is the supervisor for that person. Everybody else gets added as middle authors, which is seen as less prestigious. There can also be several authors that share first and/or last authorship, which can be marked with an asterisk behind the names and then a footnote saying that they contributed equally. Still, being the first of the shared first authors is generally considered better than being the last of the shared first authors. However, these informal rules differ between fields and journals. For example, in some fields all authors are simply listed in alphabetical order.

While being a first author can give you more credit, it also comes with more work. Usually, the first author will be the person who has done the most analyses and has written the first draft for the paper. The first author will then also incorporate all the corrections suggested by the other authors. She or he will then also reformat the paper for each submission to a journal and update the paper according to the reviewers' suggestions. This means that the difference in workload between a first author and a second author by order can be quite dramatic, even in cases where they are both technically shared first authors. If you want to be the first author on a publication you can probably increase your chances by, for example, writing the first draft of the paper. If you do not want the extra workload (and there are other possible first authors), you can lay low and see if somebody else takes the lead. Still, there can be a lot of politics involved in deciding the author list, and supervisors can have very different criteria for deciding the order.

The process from having a first draft to a final article usually takes a lot more time and effort than you think. First, you need to write a draft that you are happy with. Then, you will usually send the draft to your supervisors for commenting. Normally, your supervisor(s) will have a lot of comments – do not get discouraged if the entire paper is marked red. You will then revise the paper according to their comments and repeat the process until both you and your supervisors are happy with it. Thereafter, you will normally send the article to any co-authors for more comments and once again revise it accordingly. This entire process can be very tedious – do not be discouraged if you suddenly find that you have sent your first paper back and forth twenty times.

Eventually you will have an article version that all co-authors are happy with (or so tired of that they do not care anymore). Then it is time to submit the paper to a journal. Usually, your supervisor will have ideas on where to send it. Commonly, you aim high the first time you submit a paper, meaning that you send it to a journal with a relatively high impact factor (a metric of how often articles in a journal are cited). Impact factors for journals differ considerably between fields, but in my field of statistical genetics it seemed like the most prestigious journals had an impact factor have over 20, over ten was considered quite good, and over three was acceptable. However, researchers disagree as to how much it matters. Getting articles in high-profile journals will look better on your CV if you stay in academia, but people outside of academia may not have heard of any scientific journals. Other than impact factor, researchers may also prefer different journals depending on who they target. For example, in my field, some journals target all researchers in the natural sciences, some are more targeted towards medical doctors, some towards pre-clinical researchers. Sometimes, cost is also considered as the article authors will usually have to pay a certain amount to the journal for the article to be published. In my experience, such costs are normally paid using money from a grant, and you should not have to pay for it with your own money.

The process of submitting an article can also be daunting. Oftentimes, journals will have very specific formatting requirements, which can usually be found on their website under a heading called "author guidelines" (or similar). The requirements can be quite specific, so I would recommend deciding on a journal *before* you write up the article (although your supervisor might be of a different opinion). For example, some journals have strict word count restrictions, whereas others accept articles of any length. Some journals want the methods section to be between the introduction and the results section, other journals prefer that the methods section is last. Sometimes, you are only allowed a certain number of figures or tables, but you can often include a supplement with any figures or tables that did not fit in the main section of the article. The submission process will be a lot easier if you have conformed to these guidelines from the start. It will also make your life a lot easier if you look over other articles similar to yours in the suggested journal before you start writing. If your supervisor is open to suggestions about where to submit a paper, you can try and steer it towards journals with less restrictive formatting requirements.

After you have a paper ready to be submitted, you and your supervisor also need to decide whether to publish it on a pre-print server first or not. A pre-print server is an online website where authors can deposit their non-peer-reviewed papers, which will then be readable and citable by others. Some common pre-print servers are arXiv, bioRxiv, and medRxiv, but pre-print servers are usually field-specific. The benefit of uploading your paper to a pre-print server is that your research will be available to the research community quicker, since the review process can often take months or even years. You will also have "marked" your territory, meaning that you are not "as scooped" if somebody publishes a similar paper. You can also reference your paper and include it in your CV, which might be good if you will be applying for jobs or grants. The main downside with uploading papers to pre-print servers is that some journals do not accept papers that have already been made available (even if it is only on a pre-print server), so make sure to check before you upload. In addition, there is the theoretical problem of somebody stealing your idea and submitting it elsewhere, but in such a case it would be clear that you authored the paper first.

After you have submitted a paper to a journal, there are several possible outcomes. It can be rejected straight away by the editor, in which case you usually hear back from the journal within a few days or weeks. If it is not rejected immediately, it usually goes out "on review". That means that the paper is sent to, usually, two or three independent researchers in your field. They will then have a few weeks to look over your paper and write a review of it. Currently, researchers are generally not paid for reviewing papers and get little to no credit for it. Hence, it can be difficult for journals to find researchers willing to review papers and the process can be dragged out for many months before the editor have heard back from enough reviewers.

You will hear back from the journal after the editor have heard back from the reviewers and made a decision about your paper. The best-case scenario is that your paper is accepted as it is, but this is rare. More likely, it is rejected, or they say that they will consider it if you address the comments from the reviewers. You will also be given a deadline to get back to them.

The reviewers will usually have written a short summary of your article. They will then have listed all the things that they are not happy with. It can be large, general issues, such as "poorly written", or it can be very specific things, like "fix the typo in daibetes to diabetes on page 12, line 132". You are then expected to address the concerns raised by the reviewers, usually in a track-changes document or similar. You will usually also write responses to each reviewer suggestion in a separate document. In my experience, you usually address all the "simple" things, unless the reviewer is wrong. For the things that may take a considerable amount of time to address, you do them if they seem warranted. Does the reviewer actually have a good point here? If they do not, or if it is a change that would take many months to address and that is not crucial for the paper, you and your supervisor might choose not to do those changes. In those cases, it is common to at least acknowledge the point made by the reviewer and add a few sentences about the potential limitation in the paper, or at least politely explain why you disagree with the reviewer in the response letter.

After you and your supervisor are happy with the response, you resubmit the paper. Sometimes, the editor will decide whether to accept it or not right away, but they might also resend the updated article and your responses to the reviewers. Hence, it is usually a very bad idea to be rude to the reviewers in your responses to their comments, even if they have misunderstood something or you think that they are wrong.

As a fun fact, it is generally said that reviewer number two is always the one who is the most critical (which was generally the case with my articles, too).

The process of reviewers giving comments and you responding is sometimes repeated several times before the paper is either accepted or rejected. After formal acceptance, the paper will be sent to the editing team at the journal. The corresponding author – the one who has done the technical submission – will be sent details for how to pay for the publication. Thereafter, you will normally be sent the paper for final proofreading. Only some edits are accepted by the journal at this stage, such as correcting misspelled author names. It is therefore important that you have proof-read your manuscript at every stage of the publication process. The turn-around time at the final proof-reading stage is usually only a few working days, so make sure that you check your e-mail and spam folder frequently. After some additional days, weeks, or months depending on journal, your article will be published, sometimes years after the first article draft. Congratulations!

If your results are very novel or of interest to the general public, your department/institution might issue a press-release about your article. In these cases, journalists might contact you or your supervisor, depending on who has been listed on the press release. It has also become increasingly popular to "advertise" new papers on social media such as Twitter. Usually, the social media post will contain the main results of the paper and its implications. A social media post can greatly increase the number of people who reads your paper as well as help expand your professional network, so check with your supervisor if this is something that you want to do.

Finally, be aware of scams. Predatory journals are scam journals that basically accept all articles but have steep publishing fees. They often contact researchers with flattering e-mails asking for new articles or commentaries. A paper submitted to a predatory journal does not undergo the normal, rigid, peer-review process and your article would not be indexed in the trustworthy academic data bases. To make it difficult, normal journals may also invite talented researchers to contribute a paper or commentary to the journal by e-mail. If you are in any doubt, look up the journal's reputation and the sender online and ask your supervisor before you respond or click on any links in the e-mail.

Issuing corrections and retracting articles

Let us say that you realize that you have made a mistake in a publication, or that somebody else notices it and contacts you. What happens then? Commonly, you and/or your supervisor will contact the journal after having notified all the co-authors. You will then write a correction with a short description of what the error was as well as any updated results. This correction will then be published in the journal linked to the original article. Corrections are quite common and can be about everything from mistakes in the author affiliations, citations, or mistakes in the actual analyses, as long as they do not dramatically alter the conclusions of the paper.

Articles can also be retracted. Articles can be retracted either by the journal, or by some or all of the authors. The journal and/or the authors will usually issue a statement describing why it has been retracted. A common reason for an article to be retracted is that there is suspicion of research misconduct, such as falsified data. In rare instances, articles can also be retracted (rather than corrected) in the case of severe mistakes. However, from what I have seen this usually only happens when the mistakes were grave enough to completely change the conclusions of the article. Sometimes, the authors may carry out additional experiments to establish whether the original results are likely to be true or not.

If you think that you have made a mistake in a publication, talk to your supervisors about how to proceed.

Reviewing papers

You may be surprised to hear that you can be asked to review other researchers' papers as a PhD student. Yet, this is quite common after you have authored your first paper.

There are a few benefits to reviewing papers. Firstly, you learn a lot by reading papers with that extra critical eye. Secondly, it will give you an idea about where the field is moving, and if you are asked to review a potential high-impact paper, you will know about it before everybody else. Thirdly, you are doing a good deed – it would be seriously problematic if nobody was willing to review papers. For me, it was also helpful to see that other researchers had made mistakes and errors in the work that they submitted, as I was very nervous about making mistakes myself.

That said, reviewing papers also takes time and you rarely get any credit for it. Personally, I opted to review a few papers, but also declined to review a couple of papers when I did not have the time.

So, what is the process to review papers like, and how should you go about it?

First, you will get an e-mail invite from the journal asking if you would be willing to review. Usually, the e-mail will contain the author list and the abstract. At this stage, read over the author list to make sure that there are no conflicts of interest, in which case you should decline. You can talk to the journal if you are unsure about what constitutes a conflict of interest, but in essence it would be cases where your impartiality could be questioned. Then read the abstract in detail and judge if think that you have the necessary expertise and time to properly review the paper, otherwise you should decline.

If you choose to accept, you will be given access to the article and all the supplementary material. The next step is basically to just scrutinize the paper. You will need to look over all the material and carefully think through all aspects of the paper. Is the research question valid? Are the methods appropriate? Are there any possible biases that have not been properly addressed by sensitivity analyses? How is the writing, is it easy to understand? Are the figures appropriate? Are there any signs of fabricated data, such as two identical figures that are supposed to be

66

different? If there are certain parts of the article that you do not have the necessary expertise to judge, such as the statistics, you should inform the editor that you cannot properly review those sections.

Usually, the journal will want a recommendation about how to proceed from you, together with a more detailed report. The recommendation may be, for example, reject, accept with major revisions, accept with minor revisions, or accept as it is.

The report usually starts with a short paragraph summarizing the article. You will then be expected to first list any major criticism and then any minor criticism. If you can, write the relevant page and line number to make it easier for both the editor and the authors. Remember that the authors have usually spent a lot of time on producing the article, so be kind and include some positive feedback and phrase negative feedback nicely. You also need to consider whether the publication is suitable for the journal – is there a good match between the article topic and the journal's target audience? High-impact journals will also often want to know if the results are "important" enough to be considered in their paper.

You will usually have a week or two to submit your report. Try and be courteous and submit it on time – nobody likes having a paper out on review for months and then have it rejected. Sometimes, the editor may also ask you to review the paper again after the authors have addressed the comments from you and the other reviewers.

Conferences

Conferences can vary considerably in size. Some conferences are highly specific, others are huge and span a wide range of fields. Which conferences you should go to depends on your own preferences, but I would recommend trying out at least one of each type. Researchers also have different reasons for attending conferences. For example, they can go to conferences because they want to learn more about a particular topic or learn about the latest research in their field. They can also go to conferences because they want to advertise their own research, for example by giving a poster presentation or a talk. Finally, researchers also go to conferences to network, to travel, or to just get a short break from the daily routines.

Whatever your reason is for attending a conference, you should first try and get funding to attend the conference. Most conferences tickets cost money, and in addition you need money for travel and hotel expenditures. At some universities, your scholarship may have allocated funding for attending conferences, or there might be general funding that you can apply for. Some professors are also happy to pay for relevant conferences for their students. In some cases, conferences may have funding that you can apply for if you fulfill specific criteria.

You might want to consider submitting an abstract to the conference in the hope that you will be selected to present your research. When you submit an abstract to a conference, it can usually be selected for a talk, a poster, or not at all. Most conferences will have guidelines for the abstract format on their website together with the deadline for submitting abstracts. Conference abstracts are generally quite similar to journal abstracts. However, be aware that you may not be allowed to submit the same abstract to several journals and conferences for copyright and plagiarism reasons. Many journals even require you to inform them – and in certain cases get their permission – if you want to submit work included in an article to a conference. Some conferences also do not accept material that has been published or presented previously in any form, or only allow very recent research to be presented. Always make sure that you read and follow the instructions for journals and conferences.

There are several benefits to giving conference presentations. First of all, you start to make a name for yourself and get to talk to people about your research. The questions that people ask can give you new ideas for your research or highlight potential flaws. You can also include both oral and poster presentations in your CV and it is considered very prestigious to be invited to give a talk. Many conferences also give awards for the best talks and posters, and often have special categories for junior researchers. The downside of doing presentations at conferences is primarily that it takes time, especially if you want to do it well. For more information about how to give a good talk or make a good poster, see the sections "Giving talks" and "Making posters".

It is very easy to get overwhelmed at conferences, especially at large ones where there are several talks, seminars, and workshops at any given moment. My best advice here is to plan ahead. Look over the schedule and decide beforehand which events you will attend. Remember to allow some breathing space in your schedule so that you do not get too exhausted to take in new information.

Many students also want to tourist the city that the conference is situated in, but you will rarely have the time and energy to do that while the conference is on. Instead, I would recommend that you consider taking a few days off before or after the conference for touring the city. However, check the regulations beforehand as some funding sources only allow you to travel to and from a conference on the days adjacent to the conference dates.

If you are towards the end of your PhD, consider bringing a few copies of your CV to the conference. Companies will often have booths at the conference and might be looking to hire, or you might meet a professor with a research group that you might want to join for a post-doc.

Finally, be wary of any conference invitations that you receive in your e-mail inbox. Just as there are scam journals, there are also scam conferences that invite researchers to give talks and then charge high conference ticket prices. However, real conferences can also invite researchers to give talks by e-mail. If in doubt, talk to your supervisor and carefully look up the conference and the sender online before you respond or click on links in the e-mail.

Giving talks

Few people enjoy giving talks. Yet, you will most likely have to do a presentation for your final thesis defense, and it is a very valuable skill to master regardless of what post-PhD career you want. Giving talks becomes easier the more you practice, so try and get regular practice throughout your PhD. While different tips and tricks work best for different people, I have listed the tips and tricks that really worked for me below:

1. Create a nice standard layout

Many PhD students tend to have a very simple layout of black text on a white background when they present in group meetings. Consider having a slightly more professional (but simple) background layout, for example the official template for your department/institution. Once you have created a standard layout for a front page, middle pages, and any conclusion or acknowledgements slides, you can re-use it for all your presentations. To re-use it, either make a template in your presentation software or just have a generic presentation that you resave when you make a new presentation. Having a standard professional layout will make you both feel and look more competent and will save you time from having to individually design your more important presentations later.

2. Shorter is better – do not exceed the time limit!

For some unclear reason, many people tend to make their presentations longer than the instructions say. I find this strange, considering it means that you have to review and practice more material, might bore the audience, and feel more stressed when you give the presentation.

Instead, opt for a slightly shorter presentation than what the instructions say. You will then have time to talk slowly and clearly and time for questions at the end. In addition, the audience will likely appreciate it – do you prefer it when your colleagues finish their group meeting presentations before or after the group meeting was supposed to end?

3. Know your audience

Before you make your presentation, you need to consider your audience. If it is a presentation for people outside your field, or for the general public, you will likely need to simplify things a lot more than you think.

4. Make headings declarative

It is very common to see headings like "Introduction", "Methods", "Results", etc. However, headings that are specific and declarative will convey your message better. For example, instead of writing "Methods", you could write "Hormone X was measured using method Y" instead. Instead of writing "Results", you could write "Hormone X is associated with risk of cancer". It will make your audience better prepared to listen to what you have to say, and they will usually remember your talk better.

5. Make it as easy as possible for your audience

The easier it is for the audience to follow-along, the more of their attention they can allocate to your message. You will make it a lot easier for your audience if you have a single key point per slide, which is stated in the heading. If you have a lot of "supportive" facts for your message, consider adding them bullet point per bullet point using animations (or just several slides that add one bullet point on each slide). You can make it even easier for your audience to follow along by making the point you are currently talking about in black font and all the other bullet points in gray. If you are giving a very long presentation, you can consider having a presentation outline slide between different sections, where you highlight which section you will talk about next.

6. Write as few words as possible

One of the most common mistakes people do when giving presentations is to have too many words on their slides. Even though an audience cannot read and listen at the same time, you will often see several full sentences after each bullet point. In these cases, the audience will often just read the slides rather than listen to the presentation. Instead of writing full sentences, try and shorten each bullet point as much as you can without it getting ridiculous. That way, your audience will read the slide in a few seconds and then pay full attention to what you are saying.

7. Have a lot of empty space on your slides

Following the recommendation to have few words on your slides, also make sure that you have a lot of empty space on your slides. This will make your readers more interested instead of scaring them away with too much information.

8. Avoid abbreviations

For you, all abbreviations make perfect sense. Unfortunately, this is rarely the case for your audience, unless it is a widely accepted abbreviation. For example, if you are giving a presentation about coronary artery disease at a coronary artery disease conference, using a standard abbreviation like "CAD" for the disease is usually not a problem. However, do your best to avoid abbreviations that you have come up with yourself. If you absolutely have to such abbreviations, make sure to write them out at first mention and to emphasize what they mean in your talk.

9. Identify and stop using your default filler words and repetitive movements

Some people add "um" in every sentence when they are nervous, others just keep talking. Other people gesture wildly with their hands or bite their nails. Know what your default problems are when you become nervous and practice not doing them so that you seem confident and competent.

10. Have a summary slide at the end

A summary slide gives you the opportunity to repeat your key messages and makes it more likely that you audience will remember them.

11. Practice, practice, practice

In my opinion, there are two good ways to prepare for a presentation. You can either learn a complete script so well that you can actually "act" when you give the presentation. That is, you know the script so well that you can add pauses, smiles, gestures, and other things to make it seem natural. The other way is to learn roughly what you want to say and speak naturally. Personally, I favor the first option for presentations that are extremely important, such as the presentation part of the interviews I had for my PhD programs. For less important presentations, such as those I gave in group meetings, I went with the second option.

When you practice your presentation, make sure to speak out loud and to other people *before* you have learned the presentation by heart. It is easier to detect long, convoluted sentences that do not work if you practice aloud and giving the presentation in front of an audience can also highlight what needs to be changed. After you have a final presentation script, practice as much as you need to until you can give the presentation in a natural way without having to read from your notes.

12. Anticipate and prepare for questions

It is common to get at least a few questions throughout or after your talk. While it may be impossible to prepare good replies for all possible questions, there will usually be a few "obvious" questions. If you just prepare good replies for the obvious questions, it will make you come across as more competent without too much extra work.

13. Make sure that the technique is working beforehand

Do you have the right connecting cable between your laptop and the projector, and have you checked that it works? Are your computer batteries charged? Do you have internet connection, if needed to access your presentation or any websites? If possible, check that these things are working before you give your talk, and consider having a back-up system for important talks.

14. Get feedback

Try and get feedback after you have given a presentation! It is scary to ask for feedback, but it will help you improve. For example, you can send a chat message or an e-mail to your PhD colleagues after group meetings and ask if they could please tell you a thing or two to improve for next time.

Making posters

Posters are a popular presentation format at conferences. In brief, it is a big poster presenting a research project that is put up somewhere in the conference venue. At large conferences, there can be hundreds of posters lined up next to each other, usually for about a day or so. Quite often, there will be scheduled hours for when a designated author will stand by their poster to answer any questions from people who pass by. However, most of the time you will not be standing by your poster, and it will have to speak for itself.

If your abstract has been selected for a poster presentation, you first need to consider the poster format. What is the required poster size, and will the poster be hung in landscape or portrait format? Unless it is a digital poster, you will also need to print your poster and physically bring it to the conference. Sometimes your department/institution will have a preferred printing service that they use, or the conference might offer this service. Be aware that it can take a few days for your poster to be printed. It might also be good to allow some extra time for printing mistakes – it is not uncommon to realize that the poster size that you sent to be printed did not match the poster size that you asked for. At the printing service, you will also have to decide what your poster should be printed on. Usually, the cheapest option is glossy paper. The second cheapest option is usually matte paper, which will not reflect light as much and might be easier to read. The most expensive option is usually fabric, which is normally more durable and easier to store, so this option might be best if you want to save your poster long-term. In general, it seems that glossy paper is most common, and it works quite well in my experience.

So, how do you create a professional poster?

1. Consider learning a professional graphics software

While your standard presentation software may be sufficient make a poster, you can also consider learning a professional vector graphics software (such as Inkscape, Adobe illustrator, or Affinity Designer). Although professional graphing software may have steep learning curves, they also have a lot of useful features and the end results are often very nice. I took a data visualization course and learned Inkscape at the end of my PhD, and in hindsight, it would have been very useful to have taken that course in the beginning of my PhD.

2. Decide what the aim of your poster is

Many times, the aim of a poster is to get the other conference attendees to read the paper underlying the poster (which may or may not be published). However, you may have another aim, such as connecting to researchers in your field, getting feedback on your research from other people, or meet potential employers. Before you make your poster, consider what your aim is and make your poster accordingly.

3. Look at other posters

There are a lot of posters available online. Just search for "scientific posters" and then look at the image results. Ask yourself which posters you would be most inclined to actually read. How do those poster layouts compare to the others?

4. Think of it as a teaser, not a manuscript

If you have been to a conference before, think back to what posters you were most likely to read. Was it the posters with a lot of text and information, or those with less? For most people, it will be the posters that seemed easier to read – that is, those with relatively little information. At a conference, most people will be passing by hundreds of posters from a few meters away, and your poster needs to stand out to make people actually stop and read it.

Many doctorate students simply re-use a poster layout from an older colleague when they have to make a poster. However, *most posters at conferences are quite bad!* Many posters are extremely information dense, with almost the entire poster covered with tiny text and figures. Remember, people will usually make the choice about whether to stop and read your poster or not in a second or two. Hence, you need to have a captivating title and a layout that gives the passers-by a feeling that it is easy to read. To achieve this, think of your poster as a teaser to the manuscript, not as a condensed version of the manuscript.

5. Determine your key message

What is your main finding? Focus on that main finding. A poster is not the place to include all the sensitivity analyses that you have done, although sometimes you might want to add a single bullet point or two about them.

6. Sketch the layout on paper first

After you have determined what your key message is, start to sketch out how you would like your poster to look on ordinary paper. The main reason for doing it on paper first is that it is usually a lot quicker than doing it digitally.

7. Consider the layout and reading order

Most posters are structured with information under four headings: introduction, methods, results, and summary. While you can be creative and improve on this structure, it is not too bad of a structure, and you can definitely use it as a base. After you have decided on how you are going to organize the information, you need to decide on how to convey the information (figure or bullet points), how much information to include, and where to put the information.

Many people will read from top to bottom and from left to right when reading a poster, but reading orders differs between cultures. In addition, item size and whether an item consists of figure or text also affect reading order. To make it easier for those reading your poster, make the reading order as clear as you can. You can even use a combination of clear headings, arrows, and/or different shades to indicate reading order – be creative but clear.

8. Get started with making the actual poster

Many universities have standard poster templates that you can use. If not, just make an empty canvas in the software that you plan to use. Double-check that the size and format settings are correct before you get started.

9. Map out where to put the information and where to put the white space

If you searched for posters online and considered which ones you would like to read, you most likely realized that you were drawn to posters with a lot of space on them. "Dead space" makes your poster more inviting to read. To make sure that you do not crowd your poster too much, start with making simple empty boxes for each text and figure section. Then place them on your canvas and make sure that there is still a good amount of white space around each box.

Also, remember that your poster will (usually) be printed. Poster printing is not a perfect art, so if you have color all the way out to the border it may not be printed perfectly and leave you with white trimmings. I would therefore recommend that you have a white border around your poster so that any printing mistakes are less visible.

10. Have easy-to-read fonts and large font sizes

Sans-serif fonts are usually easier to read on posters than serif fonts. Larger font sizes are easier to read than smaller font sizes. The only information you should have in smaller font sizes is the information that most people will not read but which has to be there, such as (potentially) author affiliations, conflicts of interests, and similar information.

11. Make the title stand out

To make your title stand out, consider having a witty title that state what your findings are or phrasing the title as an interesting question. For example, let us say that you have investigated how fruit consumption affects waist-hip-ratio, which is commonly compared to having an apple- or pear-shaped body. Then, the title could be "Fruit intake determines if you become an apple or a pear" or perhaps "Will eating more fruit turn apples into pears?".

12. The title needs to be easy to read

To make your title easy to read, it needs to be short. It also needs to use simple words and avoid any abbreviations that you are not confident a clear majority of the conference attendees know. You also want to use a very large font size. Everybody, including the old professor emeritus/emerita, should be able to read it from several meters away.

13. Figures make posters easier to read and are good for conveying information

A figure of your main results is great, but figures can also be great for giving the background and explaining the methods that you have used. Once again, be creative! However, remember that your figures also need to be easily understandable, just like the rest of your poster, with easy-to-read fonts and large font sizes.

Always use vector graphics for all images, or at least make sure that they are in *very* high resolution. Posters are printed in a large format, so images with poor resolution will look terrible.

14. Have text in short bullet points

Huge chunks of text tend to scare off people. Therefore, consider using 2-3 bullet points instead under each heading, similar as you would in a presentation but written as short sentences. For the methods section, make sure that you go into the right amount of detail. For example, you would usually want to include the sample size and the main method that you have used, but you would likely not need to include details about exact settings and sensitivity analyses.

15. Add information on how to find the article, if applicable

If your poster is based on an article that is published, either as a pre-print or in a journal, always make sure that it is easy to find based on the information on the poster. For example, you could add a QR code or a digital object identifier (doi). You can also consider having the same title for your both your article and your poster.

Social media

More and more prominent researchers have a social media presence where they discuss new research, share interesting articles, and announce job openings. Whether you are a fan of social media or not, you may want to consider starting to follow the top researchers in your field on Twitter and/or Facebook. I was quite skeptical at first, but social media can be a great way to hear about ground-breaking new articles. It can also be very informative to read the informal debates and discussions between top researchers in your field. Finally, you can also "advertise" your articles on social media to get followers and increase your professional network. Still, whether researchers spend time on social media or not – and which platform they use – vary by field, so talk to senior colleagues to find out which ones to use.

Research ethics

Ethics... Few PhD students seem enthused to think about research ethics. Yet, it is crucial that you conduct your research in an ethical way, and some unethical practices are easy to do by accident. In addition to being morally wrong, being caught could result in you being expelled from your PhD program and having a ruined reputation. While the full list of unethical research practices is long, here are some things to think about:

1. Protect yourself

Sometimes it can be very difficult to know if something is unethical or not (as described below). In these cases, I would first of all recommend that you ask your supervisor in writing. Make sure that you get a written confirmation that it is okay to do as suggested. Obviously, if it is something that is obviously unethical – or potentially serious – I strongly recommend that you ask for a confidential meeting with whoever is responsible for either ethics or students at your department/institution and ask them how to proceed.

2. Have all your data and ethics applications in order

Human and animal data almost always require ethics applications before data collection. Even if you get data from another research group it may require data transfer agreements, and publicly available data usually comes with a fine print. Ethics applications, data transfer agreements, and terms of use are often highly specific and only allow the data to be used for very specific research questions. Hence, make sure that you are actually allowed to produce and use the data for your specific research question before you start your research.

Technically, making sure that all the bureaucracy is in order is normally the responsibility of the supervisor. However, that does not mean that you could not be blamed, especially if your supervisor decides that they would rather sacrifice a PhD student than themselves. So, make sure that you read and follow any regulations and agreements. If you are unsure about whether something is allowed or not, make sure that you, at the very least, get written confirmation from your supervisor that it is okay and/or check with another senior person at your department/institution (see point number one above)

3. Store your data correctly

Some data can be very sensitive, for example because it includes personal information or contains potentially hazardous information. Sometimes, you may have gotten the data in confidence from another research group, and you or your professor may have signed a specific data access agreement. Make sure that you follow any contracts and local regulations in regards to storing and handling your data. Remember to not print sensitive information. Do not leave your computer logged in when you are not there. Have unique passwords for the sensitive data. Always consider the worst-case scenarios – what could happen if somebody stole your computer, read the file you had open while having lunch, or stole those documents you left on my table?

4. P-hacking, cherry-picking, and other common misconducts

There are unfortunately several common ways that researchers try and distort their findings to get the results that they want, and you should not do any of them. P-hacking refers to the practice of redoing analyses in slightly different ways until you get a significant result. For example, adding or removing covariates in an analysis or changing the analysis method until you have a combination that give you the "desired" results. Similarly, cherry-picking results is when you highlight the few results that strengthen your hypothesis in your paper, but do not mention the results that weaken it. Even worse is to deliberately omit results that gives evidence against your hypothesis.

If you had planned to do your analyses on a thousand samples, but you do preliminary analyses after each additional hundred samples, you cannot stop your experiment when you reach the desired significance threshold. The reason for this is that you will be more likely to reach the significance threshold *at least once* if you check continuously due to chance. Similarly, you should not decide to exclude data points post-hoc, just because removing them will make your results significant.

In essence, think through a good approach *before* you start your experiments, rather than redoing experiments until you get the "best" results and then justify that approach post-hoc. If you are unsure about what the best approach may be, consider doing a smaller pilot study first where you try out the different approaches that you are considering.

5. Do the necessary sensitivity analyses and discuss potentially serious limitations

Consider the following scenario: the main analysis in your current research project gives evidence in favor of a remarkable result. However, a part of you wonders if it might be due to unspecific antibodies, rather than a true effect. If it is a possibility, it is your responsibility to make sure that you either do the required sensitivity analyses or give the potential problem its rightful attention in the discussion section of the paper. In general, try to have the mindset of *trying to prove yourself wrong* rather than trying to prove that you are right.

6. Do not plagiarize

Unintentional plagiarism is common. You might have copied a piece of text from an article, and then forget that you had not written it yourself. You might forget to reference a key source in a paper. It is even possible to self-plagiarize – when you re-use text that you have written yourself for several articles and/or your thesis. To avoid this issue, consider always putting quotation marks around everything that you copy/paste. You can also submit any articles or your thesis to a plagiarism-checking software, but make sure the software is not a scam before using it. Also, remember that many figures are under strict copyright and cannot be re-used without the copyright-holder's permission, even if you cite them. There may even be restrictions on images that you have produced if they have been published in a journal, so check with the journal before reusing them.

7. Do not steal other people's work

Is some of the work that you are including in your article actually the work of the master's student that was in the lab last year? Or maybe your work builds on the work of a post-doc that has since left the lab? If some of your research builds on somebody else's work, that person should get credit.

8. Do not ever falsify results

Never, ever, fabricate results.

It is okay not to have remarkable results. It is okay to have null results. It is also okay to make mistakes. However, it is not okay to deliberately twist the reality to your liking. Science is a continuous effort to advance humankind. Publishing false results could lead to tons of money and time down the drain as other researchers follow up on your data. These are resources that could have been spent on other research that would benefit the world. In addition, some fabricated data might inflict unnecessary damage to humans and/or animals in follow-up experiments. Do not do it.

The thesis

Whether your thesis needs to consist of published articles or is a standalone document, you should have it in mind from the start of your PhD. Thesis structures differ dramatically between countries, universities, fields, and depending on personal preference. Often, a thesis is a mix between a scientific article and a book, with a general introductory chapter, a general methods chapter, a few research chapters covering specific research projects (each having an introduction, methods, results, and discussion section), and a general discussion chapter. However, since thesis structures can vary significantly, you need to know the formal and informal thesis requirements at your specific department/institution. Hence, only use the tips below that are relevant and useful for you:

1. Read through the thesis requirements before you even start your PhD program

How many articles do you need to have published or submitted before you can submit your thesis? What is the minimum and maximum word count for your thesis, and does the word count include references and appendices? How wide do the document margins have to be? Can you include work done by others, and if so, to what degree? Do the different chapters need to concern the same subject, or do you have some leeway?

By knowing the exact thesis requirements, you can plan your PhD accordingly. If it is very strict that your thesis chapters must concern the same topic, maybe you should not take on that non-related project your supervisor is suggesting. If the paper margins have to be large, your figures will need to be narrow, and you can make them small enough to fit from the beginning. Knowing the exact requirements helps you to focus on the projects and tasks that bring you closer to having a complete thesis.

You should have been informed where you can find thesis regulations for your department/institution when you started. If you are not sure where to find them, other students or your PhD program administrator should be able to help you.

2. Skim through a completed thesis or two in the beginning of your PhD

Try and get your hands on a thesis or two from your department/institution, ideally concerning a topic similar to your own, in the early stages of your PhD. Usually, you could ask your supervisor or senior colleagues if they have any that they would be willing to send you. Otherwise, they are often available through your university library. You do not have to read through the theses in detail. Just skim through them to get an idea of how previous students have organized their theses. The point of doing this is to make the thesis writing less daunting and to get an even clearer idea of the end goal.

3. Quantify the structure of previous theses

After you have gotten a general sense of a few theses, you should quantify the various parts of them. How many chapters are there in total? Is there a separate methods section or not? How many research chapters are there? How many words are there in a typical research chapter, and how are the words divided between introduction, methods, results, and discussion? Take advantage of your text editor's word count feature.

Once again, the purpose of doing this is for you to know exactly what is required to have a good-enough thesis to graduate.

As an example, at the department where I did my PhD, the upper word limit for theses was 50,000 words, excluding references and appendix. The theses that I read from my department all seemed to be above 43,000 words. While there was no strict lower word count according to the regulations that I found, it seemed like it would be good idea to make the thesis at least 43,000 words. The introductory chapters in the theses that I read tended to be between 7,000 to 12,000 words long. Most of the theses had a separate methods chapter, but not all of them. Thereafter, most theses had between three to five research chapters, which varied in length between 4,000 to 20,000 words. However, a senior colleague told me that they had seen at least one thesis with a single research chapter, and other theses with up to six separate research chapters. Finally, all of the theses had a short, separate discussion and conclusion comprising around 5,000 words. In addition to these larger chapters, most theses had other sections as well; abstract, acknowledgements, memorandum, publications, references, appendices, etc.

4. Write a thesis outline

Consider having a rough thesis outline that you update as you start new research projects or change your research scope. This outline will likely change considerably during your PhD, but it will help you to focus your time and effort on research projects that can be included in your thesis.

Then, write a very detailed thesis outline sometime before you start writing your thesis, but after you have done most of the analyses that will be included. In what order should you have any research chapters? How should you structure your introduction? Which methods should you write about in the methods section, and which methods should you include in any research chapters? Even if your thesis will consist of published articles, it may be wise to take a step back and see how they might fit together before you take on new projects.

There are two main purposes of the detailed thesis outline. Firstly, it will make it clear if there are any large gaps in your work that you will need to address. Secondly, it will give you a very clear writing plan for your thesis if you need to write a separate thesis.

Finally, remember that the order you did your research in may not be the best order to have it in your thesis. Unless your local thesis regulations say otherwise, it is usually better to organize your research so that it flows well rather than in chronological order.

5. Prepare figures and tables along the way

At many departments/institutions, your figures and tables are required to have a similar layout throughout your thesis if you are writing a separate thesis. Consider making it easier for your future self by choosing a good layout from the start and always make "thesis figures" that comply with your thesis regulations and layout before you wrap up research projects.

6. Consider writing your thesis as you go – but in some cases it is best not to

If you have to write a separate thesis, writing each section as you go may make the writing process easier. You will then write up sections as you have them fresh in memory, and you will not have to spend three to six months (or more) just writing at the end.

The downside of writing as you go is that you may later decide to exclude some of your work because it does not fit with the rest. If that happens, you will have spent a lot of time on something that will just be deleted in the end. You also tend to become more knowledgeable and better at writing towards the end of your PhD, which can lead to quality differences throughout your thesis if you write as you go. Finally, some supervisors will not be willing to give you feedback on your thesis until the end of your PhD. In that case, you will have written your thesis without having gotten feedback along the way, meaning you may have made the same mistakes over and over again.

A good middle way might be to just write up the methods and results sections as you finish each research project but wait with writing the introduction and discussion sections in each chapter. The methods and results sections are usually easy to write, especially if you write them when you have a research project fresh in mind. In addition, they will likely not change that much even if you improve your writing and supervisors tend to have relatively fewer comments on the methods and results sections. If you do this approach, you will already have written a considerable part of your thesis when you start the final thesis writing.

7. How much time should you set aside for writing your thesis?

This question wholly depends on the thesis regulations, thesis structure, field, project, and you. Students that need to write a separate thesis will usually need a lot more time than students whose thesis will consist of published articles. On the other hand, if your thesis needs to consist of articles, you will need to allocate extra time for the articles to be reviewed, accepted, and published. However, some institutions/departments allow one or two of the articles to be pre-prints rather than published, in which case you may need less time at the end.

Most of the students that I talked to allocated somewhere between two to five months to write a complete thesis at my department. However, the time it takes to write a thesis can vary dramatically depending on a range of factors, so you need to make an estimation based on your specific situation. I would recommend that you talk to other people at your department/institution to try and get a feeling for how long it might take. Then, if you can, add on at least a month or two so you have some extra time if needed in case your supervisors are late with providing feedback, you get writer's block, or other unforeseen delays.

8. Continue with having set routines and goals as you write

Writing every day for several hours for months is a daunting process. Even for the most dedicated and self-disciplined student, it is easy to get writer's block and/or start to procrastinate. To minimize such risks, I would recommend that you continue with having set daily routines. If you can, consider decreasing your working hours or mixing the writing with any final laboratory work. For many students, writing for more than a couple of hours a day is just too tiring and any additional time spent on it is wasted, but obviously that depends on you. Another approach could be to have a word-goal for each day to stay motivated. For example, you could promise yourself to write at least 1,500 words each day, and that when you have reached that goal you can take the rest of the day off.

9. Do not write your thesis in reading order

It is easy to start writing your thesis in the order it is to be read, which is usually a bad idea. Some sections of a thesis are usually easier to write than others. For example, the introduction is usually quite tricky to write, whereas methods tend to be easier. Hence, consider jumping between different sections. Do you have a lot of energy one day? Work on something that is more challenging. Feeling very unmotivated? Do a methods section or a figure or something else that you consider easier.

The order that I wrote my thesis in was basically:

- Methods and results sections for each research chapter

- The general introductory chapter

- The introduction and discussion sections in each research chapter

- The general discussion chapter

- The abstract for the entire thesis

The miscellaneous sections, such as acknowledgements, publications, etc., I wrote when I was feeling particularly unmotivated.

10. Once you start writing, mentally divide it up into small chunks

Writing a separate thesis can take several months. To avoid getting writer's block or depressed, I highly recommend that you mentally divide it up into smaller chunks and celebrate once you have completed a chunk. For example, you could divide it up into each chapter. Then, focus on getting the introduction section for that research chapter done, and try and avoid thinking about the rest (except when planning your writing).

11. Get feedback as you go

In an ideal scenario, you would get prompt feedback from your supervisor after completing each chapter, revise, and then get feedback on it again until you have a version that you are both happy with before moving on to the next chapter. Unfortunately, this is rarely the case as many supervisors are extremely busy and put off giving feedback until the last minute. If so, consider working on the next chapter while your supervisor is reviewing the previous one, and then juggle the two chapters so that you always have something to work on.

Sometimes, however, supervisors do not provide any thesis feedback. They might claim that they are too busy, ignore your e-mails, or perhaps you have barely had any contact during your PhD. In these cases, you need to decide on the best course of action (see the section "How to manage your supervisory relationship when things are bad"). That said, also consider reaching out to other people besides your supervisors! Other colleagues may be able to give you feedback, and you could send different chapters to different people so as not to overwhelm each person. Friends and family outside of academia may also be able to help with the proofreading. In some cases, it could also be worth hiring a professional proof-reader or buy a writing assistance software to improve the text.

12. Check for plagiarism, but do not get scammed

It is possible to accidentally plagiarize. For example, you may have copied a section from an article into your thesis and then forgotten to paraphrase it, or you may not have changed your text enough if you are paraphrasing an article that you wrote yourself. To avoid the risk of being accused of plagiarism, you could consider submitting your thesis to a plagiarism checker before formal submission. However, make sure that you do not just submit it to any service you find online. There are cases of scams, where they sell your thesis to other students who then submit it – which could make it look like you were the one who plagiarized.

The viva or thesis defense

The final stage of your PhD is when you defend your research orally to examiners, and it is usually called a viva or thesis defense. This milestone also differs vastly between universities. At some universities, this is merely a formality – the "real" test of whether your research is good enough to warrant a PhD is done more informally when you submit your thesis. At other universities, students may fail at this stage, or be required to redo the process at a later stage. At some universities, this final, oral examination is done in front of a large audience that includes your family and friends. At others, the only people present are you and your examiners. Since this milestone differs so much between universities and countries, it is very important that you know what will be expected of you. Here are a few general tips and tricks:

1. Make sure that you know the procedure

Are you expected to do a presentation about your research? How long is that presentation supposed to be, if so? How long does the thesis defense normally last at your department/institution? What are the *formal* requirements to pass it, that is, what does it actually say that you are supposed to be able to demonstrate in the examination? Are you allowed to ask for a short break? What clothes are you required to wear? Once again, you should be able to find your local thesis defense requirements through your department/institution.

In addition, I highly recommend attending other students' thesis defenses if allowed. It will give you a familiarity with the procedure and often makes it seem less scary.

2. Prepare for it throughout your PhD

Giving talks at conferences or at your department/institution, or even just presenting in a group meeting, is good practice for the thesis defense. You can even consider asking your colleagues if they can ask you questions that might come up at a thesis defense when you give presentations at group meetings. That way, once it is time for your actual thesis defense, you will have had plenty of informal practice ones.

3. Re-read your thesis

At some universities, the thesis defense can be scheduled several months after you submit your thesis. In that time, it is easy to forget parts of it, especially if you have started working with something else between your thesis submission and your thesis defense. If so, make sure that you re-read thesis to refresh your memory.

4. Prepare for the standard questions

There are some questions that are very popular amongst examiners. Make sure that you have thought about what to reply for these. You can find a list with common thesis defense questions in the appendix.

5. Look up your examiners

Your examiners are most likely to ask you advanced questions concerning topics that they are well-acquainted with. Therefore, look up your examiners before the thesis defense and make sure that you know the topics related to their area of expertise well. Something that really helped me was to watch online lectures that my examiners had given, such as inaugural talks. These lectures basically gave me a quick overview of their entire careers, without having to read through all their papers.

6. Re-read key papers

Make sure that you can refer to any key articles related to your thesis topic. To do this, either re-read the abstracts or your summaries of those papers. If there are some papers that are highly related to your thesis, make sure that you re-read them completely and understand them fully.

7. Have a mock thesis defense or two before the real one

One of the best ways to prepare for your thesis defense is to have pretend-ones, where colleagues pretend to be examiners. This will give you a feeling for what it will be like, highlight areas that you might want to read up more about, and make you less nervous when it is time for the actual thesis defense. However, I highly recommend that you have your mock defense several weeks before your real one. If it is only a few days before your actual thesis defense, you may not have enough time to address any issues brought up. In addition, if you feel like everything went wrong at the mock thesis defense, you will not have "recovered" emotionally in time for your real one if it there is too little time between them.

8. Be ready to defend all the decisions you took

Why did you choose this method over that? Why did you not do this sensitivity analysis or have that control? Why did you look at these proteins but not those? Be ready to defend all the decisions that you took during your PhD. At most universities, it is okay to admit that the decisions that you took were suboptimal, but you should be prepared to answer why you took the approaches that you did. This bit can be very tricky if you just did something because your supervisor said so without understanding why. Normally, you can figure out reasons for an approach in hindsight, but if it is obvious that you used a bad approach it might be best to just admit that and say that you would have done it differently today.

9. Practice ways to dodge questions

The purpose of the viva is to find the limit of your knowledge, so eventually the assessors should reach to questions that you do not know how to answer. This is normal, so do not get worried when it happens! When it does, practice ways beforehand to deal with it. For example, you could answer a slightly related question or give a short answer and then change the subject to a topic you know better. However, many examiners will be experienced enough to notice when you are doing these things. In these cases, a good strategy can be to admit that you do not know but offer a guess and explain the rationale behind your guess. Still, if you really have no idea, it may be best to just admit that and move on. The one thing you really want to avoid is to be confident about an incorrect answer when the examiners knows that it is wrong.

10. Make sure that you understand the question

Did the examiner just ask a tricky question that you are not sure if you understood correctly? It is perfectly fine to ask if the examiner could please repeat it. You can also reiterate the question and ask if you had understood it correctly.

11. Allow yourself time to think

It is perfectly fine to say that you need a minute to think. If the examiner asks a tricky question, you can just respond "That is a very interesting question, please give me a moment to think". Similarly, if you feel that you are completely messing up the answer to a question, you can say "Sorry, this was not very coherent, please allow me to restart".

12. Make sure that you are at your peak performance

As much as you can, make sure that you are well rested and fed before your thesis defense. If you have the time, it might be nice to go for a run or a walk before the event to get some of the jitters out. Wear comfortable clothes (that still conform to the regulations and norms at your department/institution). Make sure that you will not have a caffeine or sugar withdrawal or overdose, and that there is no risk of large personal conflicts right before the thesis defense to distract you. It might also be a good idea to bring some headache pills with you, just in case.

13. If you can, have fun

A thesis defense does not have to be hours of pain – it can actually be a fun experience. Most assessors also prefer to just have a nice chat about your research, rather than hours of cross-examination. A little smile and a few jokes can turn the examination into an informal, pleasant chat (depending on your assessors). Most examiners are keen to make you feel comfortable and want you to succeed and shine.

Planning for your post-PhD career

It might feel unnecessary to think about what you want to do after your PhD if you are still in the early stages of it. However, what you want to do *after* your PhD could affect what you should do *during* your PhD. In essence, you want to use your PhD to develop the skills that will help you in your future career. For example, if your project is about data analysis and you want to switch to industry after your PhD, perhaps you should tweak your projects to include machine learning since that is a highly sought after skill by many companies (at the time of writing). Similarly, if you want to stay in academia, it might be smart to offer your supervisor help with their grant applications, since that is a skill that you will want to master if you plan to stay in academia. If you want to work with scientific writing, you could sign up for extra writing courses and offer your help on other people's articles. Oftentimes, universities offer placements in different workplaces for interested students, which can be a great way to expand your professional network, and potentially get job offers before you graduate.

Many PhD students do not realize the full extent of their career options. It is easy to think that your only option is a post-doc in your field. However, a PhD is not a career choice, but rather a stepping stone to a range of careers, and I strongly recommend that you allow yourself to think through all your options. I have listed a some of them below:

1. Post-doctoral (post-doc) researcher

Most likely, your first thought is to apply for post-docs in your field, and you should have a good idea of what such a position would entail. However, you do not have to apply for post-docs in your specific field. It is often possible to apply and get post-docs in related fields to the one you did your doctorate in. Although it may be challenging to learn the basics in a new field, you should have learned *how to learn* things during your PhD, which means that it should be a lot easier to go into a new field than it was doing your doctorate.

If you plan to apply for post-docs later, it is normally a good idea to try and get to know several professors well during your PhD. Quite often, you will be expected to provide two or three academic references when you apply for post-docs, and your application will look a lot better if at least some of those references are professors.

2. Charity or state organizations

For example, you could work on reviewing grant applications, work in museums, or analyze governmental data.

3. Consultancy

Many large management consultancy firms are always looking for new, talented individuals, regardless of their backgrounds. Several of the large consultancy firms also want to train new employees themselves, so in my experience they seem to care less about your background and more about your "general talent".

4. Scientific writing

Regardless of your PhD topic, you will have done a lot of scientific writing by the end. If you enjoy the writing process, perhaps you should consider either working for a scientific journal or for a popular science journal?

5. Careers related to the practical skills that you have learned

Consider what practical skills that you have learned in your PhD and how they may be transferred to other careers. For example, if you have spent a lot of time analyzing data, maybe you could become a data analyst. If you have learned how to make good figures, perhaps you could become an illustrator.

Do not feel limited by the exact topic of your doctorate but think about what skills you have. For example, if you have spent your PhD in a lab growing a certain kind of bacteria and running experiments on them, focus on the methods that you have learned rather than the bacteria species.

6. University administration

For those who like organization, I have met several university administrators who made the switch from research into administration. After all, you already know how the system works.

7. Teaching

Teaching can be very fun, and you will already know a topic inside out after your PhD. Depending on the country and schools that you are considering, you might have to supplement your education with a few courses, but sometimes it is possible to start teaching right away, especially at university level.

8. Working with sales

All the equipment, chemicals, etc., that you have been using throughout your PhD need somebody who sells them, and often companies want salespeople who know what they are talking about and who can relate to their customers.

9. Changing direction slightly

There are a lot of opportunities to change direction slightly by supplementing your education with just a few courses. For example, if you did a PhD in bioinformatics, you could potentially just take a few classes in business and apply for jobs in financial analytics. If you did a wet-lab PhD, perhaps you could become the perfect lab manager by doing some courses in lab management. Be creative!

10. Switch career entirely

Are you not happy with any of the options above? It is okay to switch career entirely. You will always carry with you the skills that you learned during your PhD.

Hopefully, you now feel like you have a lot of career options. But how do you know which career is right for you?

Many universities offer free career services where you can talk to career counselors. These career services may also arrange career fairs, where companies come and present their companies and what they are looking for in potential employees. Sometimes, student organizations organize similar events targeted to specific fields. Scientific conferences in your field can also be a great way to find future employers, both inside and outside of academia. Also, do not underestimate the amount of information you can get by reaching out to people! You can always ask friends and colleagues, as well as previous group members in your research group. Human resources at companies are often very helpful, so consider giving them a call if you want to know more about what they offer and if you might be a good fit for the company. You can also consider sending your CV to head-hunters in your field.

Before you start actively searching for a new job, make sure that you have a good and updated profile on the main career websites (such as LinkedIn) and any departmental websites that you are listed on. Career websites are also great for getting ideas. Look at other people's profiles to see how they have made the switch from, for example, academia to that company that you want to work for. If you know of one company that seems like a good fit for you, you can check up their employees on career websites to see what other companies they have worked on – it is very likely that some of those other companies would also be a good fit for you. Also, remember that it might be possible to do an internship through your PhD program, which could allow you to try a career before you have to decide.

You may also want to take advantage of social media. There are many social media groups targeted to individuals working in specific fields, and I have gotten a lot of great ideas, answers, and recommendations by asking questions in such groups. You can also use social media to spread the word that you are looking for a new job – just make sure that you do not antagonize your supervisor.

Finally, some words about timing. The companies that I talked to recommended reaching out to them about a year before I would like to start. However, at many universities you may have to wait several months between submitting your thesis and having your final viva or thesis defense. Check how long you will be getting your salary or scholarship, so that you know when you will need to start your new job. If you can, consider taking some time off between your PhD and the next job. Doing a PhD and writing up a thesis is hard work, and you will likely be very tired afterwards. I had several months between my PhD and my next job, which I was extremely grateful for as it allowed me to properly recharge my batteries (and write this book!).

How to prevent and overcome common problems

Why doing a PhD is hard

There are several reasons why doing a doctorate is very tough on your mental health. Some of the main reasons include:

1. Failure is much more common when doing a PhD than in school

Almost all tasks that you are given in school and undergraduate courses are doable, and doable in the allotted timeframe. However, when doing a doctorate, it is arguably more common to fail than succeed at any given task. Lab experiments frequently fail, articles are often rejected, and research projects may be abandoned after years of work.

2. It is difficult to judge performance

Most doctorate students work by themselves, and every PhD project is different. Thus, it is usually very difficult to judge how you are doing. Are you ahead or behind? In school, you got grades and knew how well you were doing in relation to your outcome goal. Since you rarely get this feedback when you are doing a PhD, it is very easy to fall into the trap of working very long hours or on weekends to try to "get ahead". It is also very easy to judge your performance on your results rather than the amount of work that you have put in. If you have then spent a month on an experiment that fails completely, it is easy to see that month as wasted, causing you to either work even harder or start to procrastinate.

3. High amount of negative feedback and low amount of praise

Some supervisors will give you a "well done" every now and then. However, the ratio between negative and positive feedback is usually extremely high when you are doing a PhD. After all, your supervisor(s) are experts in the field, and *their role is to find as many potential flaws with your research as possible.* For me, it was a lifesaver when I realized that it is always possible to find flaws with a person's research, no matter how good they are. If nothing else, there is always additional work that you could have done.

4. It is a marathon

In school, courses are rarely longer than a term or a year. Most courses are divided up into smaller sections, and each section ends with some sort of exam. A PhD is usually completely opposite. In many cases, you will work on something for three to seven years and only have one actual exam at the end. It is very easy to start to procrastinate, either because the end seems so far away or because the vast amount of work that you must do is too daunting.

5. You are literally attempting to push the boundaries of human knowledge

Many graduate students are literally doing things that nobody has ever done before and trying to discover the truth about something that nobody in the world knows the truth about. That is inherently incredibly difficult.

As you may have realized, a lot of the tips and tricks that we have covered in this book are aimed towards reducing the impact of these issues on you, for example by increasing your chances of success by getting good research projects. However, although one of the key messages in this book is to prevent problems before they arise, it is also important to know how to handle any problems that do occur. This next chapter will further focus on how to prevent and overcome common problems that students experience during their PhD.

Maximize your support system outside your PhD

Before starting a doctorate program, you want to make sure that you have optimized other aspects of your life and maximized your support system. When things get hard – and they will – you want to have other things in your life that still gives you a sense of accomplishment, self-worth, and joy. To do this, go over the below list and try and optimize these areas before and during your PhD:

1. Sleep

Getting enough sleep is crucial for being happy and productive. The exact amount of sleep a person needs vary but try to create a routine where you get approximately eight hours of actual sleep every night. If you have trouble sleeping, consider cutting down on caffeine, limiting screen time, and avoiding working in your bed. In addition, many students do not consider the detrimental effects of "social jet lag". Social jet lag refers to the habit of going to bed later during the weekend, which makes it difficult to fall asleep in time on Sunday evenings. Basically, if you normally go to bed at ten, and then party until three on Fridays and Saturdays, that actually corresponds to a quite severe jet lag. Try and minimize bedtime differences throughout the week.

2. Eat

What you eat affects your well-being – we all know this. Give your body the nutrients it needs to work. If you cook yourself, consider making large batches of food and then freezing it in a standard serving size for cheap, nutritious food that you can defrost as needed.

3. Exercise

The kind of exercise you do is less important, just make sure that you get your pulse up a couple of times per week. Ideally, try and find something that you actually enjoy doing. However, you may also want to think twice before taking up a sport professionally, especially if it does not come with substantial long-term advantages. Competing on a professional level can take a considerable amount of time and may leave you without sufficient relaxation time each week.

4. Socializing

You need a strong social support system. If you are moving to a new city or country to do your doctorate, you may want to consider moving there a few weeks before you start to have time to settle and make friends. Many universities have clubs that you can join. Be true to yourself when you choose what clubs to join, as it should be things that you actually enjoy doing. At some universities, it can also be tempting to join too many clubs and societies if there are too many things that seem fun. However, doing too many activities each week can easily become overwhelming and lead to too little time to just relax. Try and get the balance right for you.

5. Hobbies

It is good to have hobbies for several reasons. First of all, you might get to know like-minded people and meet new friends. Secondly, they can give you a sense of accomplishment that is not dependent on your PhD. Thus, when your PhD gets tough, you can still get a sense of accomplishment from finishing that airplane model or knitting that sweater.

6. Time to relax

Most people need proper down-time to feel good as well, so make sure that there is enough space in your weekly schedule to just "waste time" as well.

7. Meditation and mindfulness

Research has demonstrated that meditation can reduce stress and increase well-being and happiness. There are many apps available that can help you get started. Consider getting into a meditation routine to increase both your resilience and your happiness.

8. Nature

Being in nature has also been shown to reduce stress and increase well-being. Even if you do not normally spend time outdoors, consider going for a walk or having a picnic in your local park regularly.

9. Have your finances in order

As mentioned in the "Money matters" section, you should generally not accept PhD positions that will not pay you enough to live on. That said, you also need to make sure that you do not actually spend more money than you make. Make a budget and stick to it if there is any risk of you overspending. Also, make sure that your budget allows for unforeseen necessary medical and dental emergencies. If at all possible, save up money to have for emergencies before even starting your PhD. That way, you will not have to worry about money if you have to take a break from your PhD program due to health reasons or if you cannot finish your thesis on time. Ideally, I would recommend having six months of living expenses saved up, although I understand that this will not be possible for many students. If you do run into financial problems, remember that many universities have hardship funds that you might be eligible for.

In addition, make sure that you have all the insurances needed in the country that you are doing your doctorate in. Which insurances you need depend on the country you are in. For example, in some countries you will want a home insurance even if you rent, and health insurance requirements differ vastly between countries. Make sure that you have all the necessary insurances before you move country so that you have continuous protection.

10. Apply for extra help if entitled to

Many universities offer extra help for students with, for example, dyslexia or attention deficit disorders.

11. Mental and physical health

Doing a PhD is hard. If possible, try and get any health issues addressed before starting. If you are moving to a new city and/or country, make sure that you get in contact with your new doctor right away. Even if you do not have any current mental or physical health problems, look up how the healthcare system works if you move country and make sure that you have healthcare insurance, if needed. You want to know how to get a doctor's appointment and how you will pay for it before you need it. It might also be a good idea to look up what help the university offers in case of, for example, mental health problems. That way, it will be much easier to get help if you end up needing it later.

12. Get a mentor

Consider getting yourself a mentor. A mentor should be somebody who is more experienced than you and who you do not have a direct working relationship with. With the latter, I mean somebody who is not your supervisor or in your research group and that neither you nor your supervisor collaborates with.

The main advantage of having a mentor is that you have somebody who is unbiased regarding your PhD and career, but who is still senior enough to offer useful advice. This person would also need to be somebody that you trust and can connect with. By having a mentor, you have somebody to turn to if you get a major problem and do not how to proceed. You have somebody that can offer useful feedback on your CV and/or personal letters when you apply for jobs. In addition, you might be able to benefit from their professional network.

Mentor-mentee relationships can look very differently, but normally you would meet up every few weeks. In your meetings, you talk about your professional development, and the mentor can offer advice if you are having problems. You should not have to pay for having a mentor – this is something that more senior people do for free out of kindness.

There are different approaches to get a mentor. Some universities have mentorship programs where they connect students with alumni. There are also non-profit organizations that offer similar schemes that you could join. Otherwise, it is also possible to directly ask somebody who you think might be a good fit for you. In my experience, most people are flattered if a student approaches them and ask if they could consider mentoring, so do not be afraid to ask. If you get a mentor, make sure to treat them politely and with respect – remember that they are mentoring you as a favor.

There are no real downsides to having a mentor, besides that it takes some time to meet up with them and send them e-mails. However, there are clear benefits if it is a good mentor-mentee fit, so strongly consider getting one for yourself.

Figuring out what the problem is

At some point in your PhD, you may realize that you have not made as much progress that you would have liked in one of your regular progress evaluations (see the section "Setting up your daily life as a PhD student"). Sometimes, it is clear what the problem is, but not always. Common reasons for lack of progress include unhelpful routines, poor work strategies, supervisory problems, procrastination, striving for perfection, being stuck with bad research projects, or mental health issues. If you are not sure what is hindering your progress, I suggest that you read all the sections in this chapter as well as the chapter "How to excel at the practical aspects of a PhD" and see what speaks to you. You can also enlist the help of your supervisor, your mentor, colleagues, friends, and family and ask for sincere input, but only ask people that you trust.

Note that I have not listed "incompetence" or "inability" as common reasons for lack of progress. If you feel that those are the reasons, I recommend reading the section "Impostor syndrome" instead. It is very unusual that a student would be unable to finish a PhD because they are not "good enough". In almost all cases there is some other, underlying problem that needs to be addressed.

Problems with your supervisor

Why supervisory problems are common

Unfortunately, it is very common to eventually have one (or several) large conflicts with your supervisor. As discussed in the "Managing your supervisory relationship" section, a PhD student's and a supervisor's interests do not necessarily align.

Your supervisor likely aims for academic success. For them, that usually means getting a lot of high-impact papers published. It means having a well-functioning group where time is spent on things that will lead to high-impact papers. It means getting large grants, which in turn gives them the means to hire talented people and/or run expensive experiments. It means building a reputation for themselves as good researchers, which in effect will allow more of the above to happen. Your primary aim is, most likely, to graduate with a PhD. You might want to publish high-impact articles, but it is likely secondary to graduating. You might also want to have a personal life, get help when you get stuck, and graduate within a reasonable time frame.

These slightly different aims between the supervisor and the student commonly cause stress for the student and result in conflict between the student and the supervisor. For example, from the supervisor's perspective, it can make sense to put students on high-risk, high-reward projects. If one out of five students succeed that will still drastically improve the supervisor's and that student's careers. However, for the four students that fail, that can be a year or more of no progress towards their thesis. Similarly, supervisors may ignore their students, especially if the students are funded by external scholarships rather than the supervisors' own funding. In these cases, the students are essentially free labor as long as the supervisor do not have to spend time on them, and such a system can be very cost-effective for the supervisor.

Doctorate students often require a lot of support and help in the beginning, with few publishable results. Towards the end of their PhD, they are usually quite self-sufficient and produce a lot of valuable results. This means that there is usually no benefit for the supervisor to encourage students to graduate. Similarly, it might be beneficial for the supervisor to try and get as much work out of their PhD students as possible, even if it impacts their health. For example, supervisors may assign more tasks to a student than what is actually possible to do in the allotted time frame.

In general, you want to avoid an open conflict with your supervisor, as there is a major power imbalance between doctorate students and their supervisors. An open conflict with your supervisors comes with several potential risks:

1. Being screamed at or bullied in other ways

Some supervisors scream at their PhD students or bully them in other ways. For example, they might become overly critical of you, degrade you, call you uncalled-for nicknames, not give you fair access to equipment, or other things. It is important that you recognize that such behavior is not acceptable and constitutes bullying.

2. No future help from your supervisors

If you have an open conflict with your supervisors, they might not be willing to help you anymore. This means that you will have to rely entirely on whatever help you can get from other group members and people that you know. However, in the case of an open conflict with your supervisor, other people may start to avoid you to not get involved in the conflict.

3. Being removed from future papers or moved down the author list

If your supervisor has no reason to keep you happy anymore, they might not include you on papers, or you might find that you are suddenly just a middle author on that paper where you were supposed to be first author on.

4. Your reputation might suffer, and you might be left without references

A poor relationship with your supervisor could damage your chances to get a good job after your PhD. Your supervisor might backtalk you to other researchers in the field or be unwilling to give you a good reference. Even if you plan to leave academia, a conflict with your supervisor might mean that you will not get a good reference when you apply for your next job.

5. You could lose access to your data or the lab

In many cases, it is the supervisor who owns your data and decides who can have access to the lab. There is therefore a hypothetical risk of your supervisor removing your access to your data or the lab. If you can and it is allowed, consider making your own copies of any necessary data and results before a conflict escalates. Still, if your supervisor removed your access to your data or the lab without a good reason, many universities would consider it active sabotage. If such a case were brought to the university's attention, the supervisor would likely risk disciplinary action.

6. It might become significantly harder to pass any exams

The amount of power that your supervisor has over your exams varies between countries and universities. At some universities it is almost impossible to pass any exams without your supervisor's blessing, as your supervisor can either formally or informally talk to your assessors. At some universities, signing up for a PhD milestone might require your supervisor's signature, which they could simply refuse to give or procrastinate with giving. Even when it is against the university regulations for supervisors to try and influence the examination process, they could have an informal chat with your examiners. In such cases, the student would likely have a strong case if they decided to report the incident, but it could be difficult to prove.

7. You could be kicked out of the group and potentially your PhD

In theory, a supervisor could expel a student from their group or even their PhD program. Whether this is an actual risk or not depends on your university regulations, and your university should have regulations that protect students from being unfairly treated.

In summary, these potential issues make conflicts with a supervisor extremely difficult and risky to navigate, and there is unfortunately no magic solution. However, there are a few things that you can do to maximize your chances of a good outcome if there is a risk of a conflict with your supervisor, which we will cover next.

How to be protect yourself against supervisory problems when things are good

Given that conflicts between PhD students and supervisors are so common, I would strongly recommend that you actively manage your supervisory relationship from the start:

1. Make sure that you do not do anything that can be used against you

If things would go bad, you do not want to have done anything that the supervisor can bring up against you. Hence, try and do everything by the book to avoid giving the supervisor any ammunition against you if things take a bad turn:

- Follow any local rules about being present at work, attending meetings, doing presentations, etc..

- Do not skip work. If the PhD situation is affecting your health, get a doctor's note about it and inform your supervisor that you will be away on sick leave.

- Do not violate any regulations, such as data security, information sharing, etc..

- Do not openly backtalk your supervisor. If you need to talk about your situation with somebody to offload, ideally do it to people outside your workplace or with people that you trust completely. If you talk about your situation to other people, avoid doing it in places where others can overhear you – maybe it is your supervisor's partner that is sitting at the table next to you.

2. Build relationships with other people in your group/field

Remember that there are other people you can get support from in addition to your supervisor. If you get to know other people in your group or department, you can turn to them for help with your projects even if your supervisor ignores you. If you know them well, you can also ask them to be your references in the future when you apply for jobs. Just make sure that you help these people back – they have no obligation to you, and you want to build mutually beneficial relationships.

3. Learn how to best say "no" to your specific supervisor

There are many ways of saying "no" to your supervisor and avoiding things that you do not want to do. You need to actively figure out which approach works best with your supervisor in order to both avoid conflicts and have an easy PhD.

For example, let us say that your supervisor has suggested a huge high-risk, high-reward project that you really do not want to do. Sometimes, you might have a supervisor that would accept a simple "no". Other times, it might work best to point out all the problems with the project to dissuade your supervisor. In other cases, perhaps it is just best to avoid working on that project and instead work on the projects that you want to do. Whenever your supervisor brings up the huge project, you can say that you will look into it and then switch the topic to the project that you like. It might also be possible to make a bad project a good one by changing it slightly. For example, if the project is too big, it might be possible to focus on a small but doable aspect of it to make both you and your supervisor happy. With some supervisors, the best approach might be to negotiate. Perhaps you can agree to work on a project some days of the week if you are allowed to work on a project of your choice the other days.

Similarly, you can also say no to overtime in different ways. With some supervisors, you might be able to just tell them that you have too much work and ask for a break. With others, it might be better to just reduce your work hours to the amount that works for you without saying anything. Other times, the main problem could be that your supervisor does not understand how much time the experiments are taking and think that you are just working a few hours a day. In these cases, a simple conversation where you outline all the separate tasks could make him or her understand how much you are actually working. Your supervisor might also be able to suggest things that could be down prioritized or offer advice on how to work more efficiently.

As you can see, there are many different strategies that you can use to get your way. Which strategy works best depends on the situation and your supervisor. However, the main take-home message is that you can say no to things, just think about how you will do it and, if possible, avoid open conflicts with your supervisor.

4. Fill out any regular progress or feedback forms properly

If your university has progress or feedback forms for you to fill out regularly, make sure that you fill them out properly. If things are progressing according to plan, you want to make that official. That way, it will be clear that you can work well under the right circumstances, something that could really speak in you favor if you end up with supervisory problems later.

How to manage supervisory problems when things are bad

Even if you have been the perfect PhD student and have done everything right, you can still end up with a supervisory conflict on your plate. If that happens to you, you can consider the following courses of action, but tread carefully! Some of the suggestions could be detrimental for your specific situation, so you need to make a judicious decision on what approach is best in your particular circumstances.

1. For very serious issues, you should involve the police and any other appropriate instances

In severe cases, such as physical or sexual abuse or harassment, you should immediately contact the police and any other relevant instances. Many universities offer specific support services for sexual violence, and you can usually also turn to relevant healthcare services. You have a right to feel safe at your workplace and should not have to deal with such things yourself.

2. Know your rights

My impression is that universities tend to side with the student when there is a disagreement between the student and their supervisor. Unhappy students could result in them dropping out or leaving bad reviews of the university. High drop-out statistics and bad publicity could damage the university's reputation and cause fewer students to apply, in effect leading to less money for them. In many countries, it could be very destructive for the university if it came out that they ignored a student's plea for help.

Because of this, most universities have regulations in place to protect the students. There are usually guidelines for how often supervisors are required to meet with their students, what support students are entitled to, and when a student have gotten far enough to be allowed to graduate. Do not just take your supervisor's word on what rights you have, as some supervisors might lie about the regulations or tell you that things are done differently in practice. Therefore, make sure that you read the regulations yourself. If in doubt on where to find them, you should be able to ask your local student representative.

Most countries also have laws in place to protect employees as well as consumer rights laws that may be relevant if you are a student paying tuition for your PhD. If needed, consider talking to a lawyer to discuss your options.

3. Document everything and gather evidence

If you are being mistreated by your supervisor or are having disagreements for other reasons, you should start to keep a secret "war journal" immediately. You want to be able to say exactly when and what your supervisor said or did things to you that could be considered immoral, illegal, or wrong. Ideally, keep evidence of what was said or done. In essence, you want to be able to tell the full story to any student representatives, professors responsible for student welfare, and in any disciplinary hearings. This could include the following, but make sure that nothing is illegal or against university regulations before you do them:

- Get e-mail confirmations of supervisory orders that you disagree with. If you have received them orally, consider writing an e-mail summary of what was said. To avoid conflict, you could just summarize it and ask if this was what they meant in a nice way. Consider saving such e-mails somewhere else besides your university e-mail account as well if there is any risk of you suddenly losing access to it.

- Save any e-mails or other communication that demonstrate any bad behavior by your supervisor, such as name-calling or bullying.

- Consider taking the names of other people that saw or heard your supervisor's bad behavior in case of a potential disciplinary hearing, for example if your supervisor behaves badly at a conference or in the university cafeteria.

- In some countries it is legal to do secret voice recordings in certain situations.

Obviously, for all of these things remember to be sure that they are legal and moral to do, and do not use the information in any illegal or unethical ways. The purpose of having a "war journal" is simply to be able to tell outsiders what has happened. Hopefully you will not have to use it – your situation could improve just by your supervisor realizing that you have kept track of what they have done.

4. Consider reaching out to other people that might have been mistreated

If your supervisor is mistreating you, it is not unlikely that other current or former students (or senior colleagues) have been or are being mistreated. However, tread very carefully when you reach out to other people that might be mistreated! You do not want to end up in a situation where the other person tells your supervisor that you are reaching out to other people behind their back. At the same time, it can be very reassuring to know that you are not alone. You can also help each other, both with your PhDs but also with brainstorming ideas of how to deal with the situation. Also, if one student makes a formal complaint, it might be because that student is a "bad" student. If several students in a research group make a formal complaint, the university will often feel forced to act and are more likely to take the students' side.

5. Quit listening to your supervisor and do your own race

In certain cases, you may be able to just finish your PhD on your own, without having any contact with your supervisor. Obviously, if you start to just focus on your own ideas, you are less likely to receive help if you get stuck. Hence, I would be careful about going down this route unless you know what you are doing and do not rely on input from you supervisor.

6. Figure out how much support you have from the university

In certain cases, you might be left with no other option than to make informal or formal complaint about your supervisor. The exact procedure to make a formal complaint differs between universities. However, usually there will be some student representatives and professors responsible for student welfare that you can contact in case of conflict. At some universities, you might already have a professor assigned as an advisor for these situations. In general, I would recommend turning to somebody that you trust first. Ask for an informal meeting, and ask for it to be kept confidential, without saying too much over e-mail. The reason for this is that you want to be able to gauge the other person's reactions. Are they siding with you or with your supervisor? In an actual meeting (rather than just e-mail), you will be able to start telling your story and see how they react before you tell them too much. Focus on the key facts calmly and try to include concrete examples of how your supervisor is mistreating you. Be sure that those issues are clearly against any university regulations. If you have evidence of their wrong behavior, mention that and offer to show it to them. In general, you want to avoid strong language or emotions. Focus on the facts and be truthful, and do not hide your own mistakes. Also, remember that the person that you are talking to likely have a lot of things on their to-do list, so be succinct. Before the meeting, also think through what you want out of the meeting. What is it that you would like them to do? If you have a potential solution, you can mention that, but consider phrasing it as a suggestion rather than an order. If you are talking to a professor responsible for student welfare, they have likely been in this situation before and might already know of good approaches to handle the situation.

7. Change supervisor

It might be possible to change supervisor. Changing supervisors can feel daunting but might drastically improve your situation. While it may feel like you will lose valuable time if you change supervisor, it can very well save you time in the long run and make your life a lot easier. This strategy is likely to be best if you experience problems with your supervisor early on in your PhD or if you have not gotten very far. However, you will likely not be able to change supervisor more than once or twice. This means that if it would not work out with your second or third supervisor, you might be stuck and have very limited options to change supervisor again.

Procrastination

Some students are prone to procrastination, others are not. However, even if you rarely procrastinate, it is very likely to happen at some point during your PhD. The structure of doctorate programs seems to encourage procrastination. You are working towards a goal that are many years into the future. The amount of work is daunting, and the daily work you put in feels microscopic compared the amount of work you will have to do. In many research groups, there are no fixed working hours, and nobody keep track of what you are doing. So, how can you minimize the risk of procrastination, and how can you get started again if you feel unable to work?

1. Treat your PhD program as a job from the start

My best advice to minimize procrastination is to treat your PhD as a regular job. Strict routines are your best ally against procrastination, yet many doctorate students work when they feel like it. However, such an approach tends to make you constantly feel like you should be working and feel guilty when you are not. This results in time off not really being time off, and you do not get the proper downtime that you need. In addition, you have to muster up motivation and energy before every single hour of work.

I therefore recommend that you set a strict work schedule, for example weekdays 8 am to 5 pm, with a one hour lunch. The hours that you decide should be a doable in the long run, so do not schedule 12 hours a day the entire week. Then, make sure that you actually start work on time – you could even ask a friend or family member to hold you accountable.

2. When you have time off, make sure it is really time off

Avoid checking your e-mail and other work-related things outside of your working hours unless you have to. Even if checking your e-mail only takes a few minutes, it will make your brain think of work for a much longer time.

3. Schedule time to do particularly unpleasant tasks.

Sometimes you might be procrastinating because of a single, particularly unpleasant task. In these cases, consider scheduling the task in your calendar at the time of the day when you have the most energy and focus.

4. Ask somebody else to give you a deadline

You can ask a family member or a friend to give you a deadline, potentially involving a bet. For example, if you do the task before a certain date, they will give you a massage, but if you do not you will have to give them five massages.

5. Schedule the next day at the end of each day

If it is difficult to get started each morning, consider planning what you will do first thing in the morning the afternoon before. You can deliberately make it an easy task, just to get started.

6. Be your own best friend

You are doing something few people would ever even consider doing. Doing a PhD is hard, and many doctorate students are extremely diligent people that are always striving for perfection. Be kind and have compassion with yourself. You are doing your best, and actually changing your attitude towards yourself from slave driver to best friend can make your life both more enjoyable and minimize procrastination.

7. Reward yourself when you have done good work

Do not forget to reward yourself after you have done an unpleasant task or reached a milestone in your PhD. Do something fun with a friend, treat yourself to a nice dinner, throw a party, or do something else that you enjoy.

8. Try and find what motivates you

While it is possible to work without motivation, it does make it easier. What made you start a PhD to begin with? You can also consider visualizing your graduation or future job, reading motivational books, listening to motivational pod casts, calculating how far you have gotten already, or see yourself enjoying any rewards that you have promised yourself.

9. Consider lowering your expectations of how much you should work

Five minutes spent on work is better than zero. Reading one article is better than reading zero articles. If you are really stuck in a procrastination mode, consider drastically lowering your expectations on how much work you will get done. Change your set work hours to an hour a day and allow yourself to be happy with that. You can always increase the number of hours later, but the important thing now is to get back on track.

In a similar way, striving for perfection can be highly detrimental to productivity. No PhD project is perfect, and they do not have to be either. At some point, you just have to decide that something is good enough and be happy with it. See the section "Fear of making mistakes and striving for perfection" for more tips and tricks.

9. Change your environment

Sometimes, a change in the environment can make wonders for your productivity. Perhaps you can go to a café, a library, or sit outdoors to read those articles or write on your thesis? Maybe you can visit a collaborating lab group for a few weeks or months to get a change of scenery and some new inspiration?

10. Sometimes, you just really need time off work!

Sometimes, procrastination can come because you are wiped out. You might have had a very hectic year, with little vacation and time off. In these cases, I recommend taking proper time off. You are not a machine and getting burned out could mean many months (or years!) before you can return to work. Therefore, schedule time off before you feel exhausted, and if you are exhausted, take at least a few weeks off. Another alternative could be to sign up for a course, internship, or something else that you will have to do anyway at some point, but that offer a change of routines.

Fear of making mistakes and striving for perfection

One of my main struggles as a PhD student was an intense fear of making mistakes. In my PhD, I did a lot of coding and analyzed very large-scale data. It seemed so easy to accidentally make a mistake that could drastically change the results of the analyses, such as misspelling a variable in my code or misunderstanding how a software or mathematical formula worked. The large scale of my analyses meant that it was impossible to double-check all my results by hand. When it became time to write articles about my findings, I was extremely nervous about accidentally writing the wrong number in the text or citing the wrong paper. Sometimes, I would wake up in the middle of the night with a pounding heart, thinking that I had made a mistake.

Another common problem for PhD students is striving for perfection. Students with this problem may be reluctant to ever finish projects. There are always better methods that could be used, more sensitivity analyses that could be done, and text that could flow better. Students with this problem tend to work long hours and still never finalize anything.

A fear of making mistakes and perfectionism can both take a lot of time and energy, as well as decrease your chances of getting your doctorate. If you have these problems, first consider going over the list in "Maximize your support system outside your PhD" to see if there is anything you can do to optimize your well-being and resilience. In addition to those tips, there are a few other things that you can consider doing:

1. Talk to trusted colleagues and friends about it

You are not alone! These are common problems. By talking to people that you trust about it, you are likely to feel calmer about it yourself. Senior colleagues have usually already made mistakes and can often calm your fears. After all, almost all mistakes can be fixed.

2. Notice the mistakes and imperfections in articles

For me, my fear of making mistakes lessened as I saw the mistakes in other people's work. Throughout my PhD, I found mistakes and problems in several high-impact papers that might even impact the conclusions. By noticing how common it is to make mistakes, you can hopefully become less worried about making them yourself. That said, you should obviously take all reasonable precautions to lessen the risk of publishing incorrect results.

Similarly, if you go in depth into any article, you will see that they are not perfect. There are always sentences that are unclear or additional datasets or analyses that would have made the article better.

3. It does not have to be perfect, just good enough

It is impossible to write a perfect article or a perfect thesis. You will never get done if you are striving for perfection. Actively try and change your mindset to striving for good enough. If you have perfectionist tendencies, striving for good enough is still likely to yield high-quality results. You can actively set a lower mental threshold for when a paper is finished, for example, when it is similar quality to a typical paper in your field.

4. You are a trainee

Ultimately, a PhD student is a trainee. You are studying to become an independent researcher, but you are not actually expected to be one yet. Hence, it is reasonable to put some of the responsibility on your supervisor. He or she is also supposed to think about potential errors or if something is not good enough to be published.

5. Mistakes can be rectified

Mistakes can happen to everybody. In my opinion, there is no shame in it, as long as you have done a reasonable effort to minimize the risk of mistake and try and correct them. If you think that you have made a mistake in a publication, read the section "Issuing corrections and retracting articles" and talk to your supervisor.

6. Determine a reasonable number of times to double-check things

You want to avoid making mistakes and double-checking once or twice is good. However, double-checking something ten times is likely neither healthy nor productive. It is not good for your mental health, and it will reduce the amount of time that you spend on actual research to benefit humankind. Hence, consider setting a limit on how many times you should double-check things and stick with it.

7. Ask somebody else to double-check if it is a crucial step

If there is something that is crucial to get correct, consider asking a colleague to double-check your work. It is usually easier to spot mistakes in other people's work than your own.

8. Decide when to double-check what parts of a project

Some things – like the main foundations of your project – is usually best to double-check in the early stages of a project, so that you do not waste months doing sensitivity analyses for a result that turns out to be a mistake. Other things, like references, are usually best to wait with double-checking until right before the final submission. There are several reasons for this:

- Large chunks of articles or your thesis are usually removed in the editing process, so you do not want to waste time double-checking text that will be deleted anyway.

- What you work on is usually not dependent on if you cited the right reference in a text or not. This means that you do not have to redo other work if you have referenced the wrong article.

- You can only double-check references in an effective way a few times. After that, your brain can no longer effectively "see" the text. Hence, if you double-check the references in a first draft too many times, you will not be able to properly double-check it at the final proof-reading stage.

9. Take a break between doing something and double-checking it

You are more likely to spot mistakes if you take a break between when you do it for the first time and when you double-check.

10. Differentiate between suboptimal and mistakes

Research is never perfect. There will always be things that you can improve. Do not sacrifice a completed, good enough project for perfect project that is never finished. Oftentimes, there are several ways to do something in research. It is easy to think that a suboptimal approach is incorrect when it is actually just suboptimal. With all likelihood, there are also benefits with your chosen approach.

11. Make sure your well-being routines are in order

Worry tends to get worse if you are stressed or if you do not get enough sleep. Make sure that all your well-being routines are in place, such as sleep, social interactions, and exercise (see the section "Maximize your support system outside your PhD").

12. Get help if needed

Many universities offer professional help for anxiety and other issues, sometimes even for free. If you find that your fear of making mistakes or perfectionism is having an impact on your well-being and health, get in touch with student support or book an appointment with your GP.

Impostor syndrome

Impostor syndrome is when you feel less competent than you are. You might fear that one day your supervisor will realize that you are a fraud, or think that everybody else is much more clever than you. Oftentimes, people with impostor syndrome attribute all their successes to external factors but berate themselves harshly for any mistakes or failures. To help with impostor syndrome, you can consider trying the suggestions below:

1. Talk to others about it

Impostor syndrome is very common amongst PhD students and academics. Consider having a heart-to-heart conversation about it with somebody that you trust. It is very likely that the other person has felt the same way, which can help you feel less isolated. If you do not want to talk to somebody else about it, consider just searching for "impostor syndrome" online to read other people's experiences of it. You are not alone.

2. Do not compare yourself to others

Avoid comparing your progress to that of others. When you compare yourself to others, it is easy to sum up everybody else's successes but disregard their failures, which you often do not even know about. Even if you compare yourself to just one person, it is easy to compare yourself with the most successful PhD student, rather than the average student. In addition, all doctorate projects are different. Some PhD students are lucky and end up with easy projects, and some end up with nightmarish ones. Therefore, you cannot make a fair comparison of, for example, the number of published articles between two students.

3. Realize that your thoughts and feelings may be lying to you

Thoughts and feelings are not necessarily true, so do not assume that any negative thoughts give an accurate reflection of reality.

4. Accept your "impostor syndrome"-feelings and thoughts, but act as if they were not there

For example, your thoughts might tell you that you should quit your PhD before anybody realizes that you are a fraud. Unless you truly want to quit, consider just accepting that thought but otherwise continue living your life as normal. Eventually, you might start to feel like you belong.

5. Consider starting a meditation and/or mindfulness practice

Once again, meditation and mindfulness practices have been shown to reduce stress and increase acceptance and well-being.

117

6. Get help if needed

If you feel that your impostor syndrome is affecting your mental health and/or well-being, consider reaching out to any services offered by your university or your GP to get professional help.

Null results, being scooped, or realizing that your project has fundamental flaws

It can be very disheartening when you have spent years on a project, just to end up with no significant results. Other times, you may be scooped, which refers to when somebody else is first with publishing research very similar to your work. Is all the time that you have spent on the project now completely wasted? The short answer is "not necessarily".

Research is a continuous process, and one study does not make a truth. Both null results and results that are the same as a previously published study can still help you towards your PhD and potentially be published.

If your graduation requirement is a distinct thesis, rather than a set number of articles, null results can often be included. You will simply need to discuss why you got null results. Is it because there is no true association, or was your power too low to detect anything? Even if your thesis needs to consist of a set number of articles, you can often still publish null results if the rest of the study is robust. Basically, if you have made sure that you have a good research question and a valid approach to testing it, you have done good research and the results should be published. It is well recognized that only publishing results that show an effect bias research. It may not be possible to publish it in a high-impact journal, but it should be possible to publish in a more modest, but still reliable, journal.

Even if you have been scooped, your results may still be possible to include in your thesis. If it is a distinct thesis, you can likely just be honest and write that the work was completed before the publication of paper X, and then discuss the differences between your work and theirs. It can be more difficult if your thesis has to consist of published articles. Still, it is quite rare for a paper to be completely scooped. Usually, there will be some differences that means that your research is still publishable, albeit potentially in a more low-impact journal. For example, if you have a used a different dataset, your study independently replicates the previous study, which is a very important part of research. If you have used the same dataset, you will need to look at the methods – are there any major methodological differences that means that your article adds something to the previous article? If not, are there any additional analyses that you could do that would be of value to the field?

Sometimes, the main problem is that you discover a flaw with your research that invalidates all the other results. For example, perhaps you discover that the bacteria you thought you were working on were a contamination, or that the antibodies did not measure the protein that you thought that they were measuring. This can be a more difficult problem to solve. If you are writing a separate thesis, you can sometimes include such results anyway. If your thesis has to be based on published articles, I recommend that you see if you can tweak the article slightly and publish it anyway. Perhaps the results are still of interest, even if they pertain to another kind of bacteria? Or perhaps you can publish it as a "watch out for this"-article? If you have made the mistake, it is likely that others might, too. Can you turn it into a methods paper, highlighting that certain sensitivity analyses should always be done to avoid the mistake that you did? In short, try and be creative and most things can be salvaged, and if they cannot, drop the project and get started on something else. Remember, doing mistakes is an integral part of doing a PhD. Most projects that I started during my PhD were dropped before completion, and only about 10% of started projects ended up being included in my thesis. With other words, it is completely normal for projects to fail. Hang in there!

Mental health

A PhD is very mentally taxing. Mental health problems are very common among PhD students, including depression, anxiety, and stress related disorders.

Even if you follow the advice in this book, you can still get mental health issues. If so, do not wait with getting help. It is easier to fix mental health issues the sooner you address them. Many universities have mental health centers that you can turn to, or you can contact your doctor. Please reach out for help before it gets too bad!

There are usually many options available for students suffering from depression, anxiety, and stress-related disorders. First of all, make sure that you get proper sleep, nutrition, and time to relax as a first step. Exercise has been shown to reduce depressive symptoms to the same extent as many drugs. Even if you do not feel like going for a run, do what you can. A walk around the block is better than no exercise at all. Time spent in nature has also been shown to improve mental health. If you are drinking alcohol or doing drugs, I strongly recommend quitting (slowly if there is any risk of dangerous withdrawal symptoms). Both alcohol and many drugs can cause depression and anxiety-related issues on their own and will likely make your situation worse. Also consider reducing your caffeine intake. A large caffeine consumption can reduce your sleep quality and cause anxiety-like symptoms. In addition, engage your support system and reach out to those close to you. Isolation can often worsen symptoms, and you need to continue to do fun things. You can also consider reducing your working hours, especially if you are working overtime. If you might be overworked, consider taking a break for a couple of weeks to recharge your batteries. It is better to take a couple of weeks off when you start to get symptoms of burnout, than having to take many months off later.

Depression and anxiety are not only caused by external factors but are also caused by chemical imbalances in the brain. Therefore, you may need medication to get better. Ideally, reach out to your doctor early in the process to discuss your options. Besides being able to prescribe medication, your doctor can also recommend therapy, and especially cognitive behavioral therapy has very good effects on many mental health issues.

Afterword

Few things will teach you as much as doing a PhD. However, while doing a doctorate is supposed to be challenging, you should not have to suffer while doing it. My hope in writing this book was to help other doctorate students better navigate the academic landscape to make their PhD journeys easier. That said, I am sure it will still feel like a rollercoaster sometimes. In particular, many students describe the middle of their PhDs as very strenuous, as they no longer feel the optimism that they felt in the beginning, have yet to learn all the skills, and graduation seems far away. Still, it is very rare for PhD students to not get their doctorate as long as they continue to show up for work and ask for help when needed.

With that said – hang in there and try to enjoy the ride!

Best of luck,

Dr. Jenny Censin

Acknowledgements

I would like to thank Mr. Peter Strain, Ms. Viktoria Rydén, Dr. Johan Henriksson, Dr. Nick Crang, and Ms. Monica Sundström, who all gave me very useful feedback on this book. Thank you!

Appendix

Example PhD interview questions

- Why do you want to do a PhD?

- What would your PhD project be about?

- Why do you want to do this doctorate project?

- Why do you want to do your PhD project with Professor X/at department Y/at university Z?

- What would be the main benefit to the world if you did this project?

- What do you perceive would be the main difficulties or limitations with your suggested project?

- What are the main assumptions in your field?

- You propose to use method X in your PhD project, how does that method work?

- What do you see as the main issues in your proposed field today?

- What are some things that you would have to learn to do this project?

- How will you fund your project/your PhD?

- What are some potential ethical issues with your proposed research?

- Why do you think that you are a good fit for this project?

- Tell us about your previous research project X?

- Can you describe how the methods in your previous research project X works?

- What were the main results of your previous research project X?

- What were the main difficulties when you did previous research project X?

- What were the main things that you learned when you did previous research project X?

- Why do you want to do your PhD in the same field as your previous research project X/why do you not want to do your PhD in the same field as your previous research project X?

- What do you want to do after your PhD?

- Tell us a little bit about yourself?

- How would other people describe you?

- What are your major strengths/weaknesses?

- What is your biggest achievement so far?

- What do you like to do on your spare time?

- Could you describe a difficult situation that you have overcome?

- Tell us about somebody that you did not get along with, and how you handled that situation?

- Where do you see yourself in 5/10/20 years?

- Could you describe some recent research that interested you that is not related to your PhD project?

- There are 50 other candidates that have applied for this position. Why should we hire you?

- Do you have any questions for us?

Example thesis defense questions
- Why did you want to do a PhD?

- Summarize your research in X minutes.

- Summarize your research so that your grandmother would understand.

- Summarize your research in a sentence.

- Why is your research important?

- How is your work novel?

- How does your thesis compare to what you had planned to do when you started?

- What results surprised you the most? Why?

- In what ways does your research advance the field?

- Which are the most important papers related to your thesis?

- Who is a key researcher in your field?

- What are some major developments that have happened in your field since you began your research?

- What are main strengths and limitations of your research?

- A key concept in your thesis is X, what is your working definition of that concept?

- Describe the history of method X/field Y.

- What would have made your research better?

- What are the main controversies in your field?

- Why did you choose this research topic?

- What are the assumptions underlying your research?

- What would you have done differently, knowing what you do today?/If you would re-do your PhD, what would you do differently?

- What part of your thesis are you most proud of? Why?

- What have you done that makes you worthy of a PhD?

- How do your findings relate to the work in the lab of person X?

- Describe a challenge that you faced and how you overcame it.

- Who is most likely to be interested in your research?

- How does your research generalize?

- How has your view of your field changed since you started your research?

- What is a recent research finding that you find very interesting that is not related to your thesis?

- What are the main obstacles in your field that hampers progress?

- Describe an ethical dilemma that you had and how you dealt with it

- Why did you choose method X? Is there any other method that would have been better? Why did you not do it using method Y instead?

- What are the main strengths and limitations to method X?

- How does method X work?

- Can the methods that you used be applied to study X (special interest of the examiner)?

- How did you collect your data?

- What is a p-value?

- What is the difference between standard deviations and standard errors?

- If you would get a grant to do research building on your thesis, what would that project be? How would you design that project?

- What do you think the main developments in the field will be in the next X years?

- What do you plan to do after your PhD?

- Will any parts of your thesis be published? Why or why not? What journal would you like to publish in and why?

- How will your findings affect future research, if at all?

- What skills that you have learned do you think will be of most use to you in the future?

Printed in Great Britain
by Amazon

79451578R00078